Food Facts and Figures

also published by Faber

VEGETARIAN STUDENT *by Jenny Baker*
THE WHOLEFOOD COOKERY BOOK *by Ursula M. Cavanagh*
THE HOME BOOK OF VEGETARIAN COOKERY *by N. B. and R. Highton*
FOOD FOR ARTHRITICS *by Judy and Jim Andrews*
FAT-FREE RECIPES *by Nevada Lampen*
MORE FAT-FREE RECIPES *by Nevada Lampen*
SUGAR-FREE CAKES AND BISCUITS *by Elbie Lebrecht*
COOKING FOR THE WAYWARD DIABETIC *by Lily MacLeod*
THE VEGAN COOKBOOK *by Alan Wakeman and Gordon Baskerville*
CLINICAL NUTRITION FOR NURSES, DIETITIANS AND OTHER HEALTH CARE PROFESSIONALS *by John Dickerson and Elizabeth Booth*

Food Facts and Figures

A comprehensive guide to healthy eating

Jill Davies
Senior Lecturer in Nutrition, Division of Home Economics, South Bank Polytechnic

John Dickerson
Professor of Human Nutrition, Division of Nutrition and Food Science, University of Surrey

LONDON · BOSTON

First published in 1989
by Faber and Faber Limited
3 Queen Square London WC1N 3AU

Photoset by Parker Typesetting Service Leicester
Printed in Great Britain by
Richard Clay Ltd Bungay Suffolk

A CIP record for this book is available from the British Library

ISBN 0-571-15273-2

Contents

List of Tables

List of Figures

Introduction

Each adult person in the UK who lives to be seventy years of age will consume about 30 tons of food in order to obtain the nutrients necessary for the growth and efficient working of their bodies. The types of foods eaten by different people will vary enormously and some diets will be more healthy than others. Certain diets are now recognized to put people at risk of ill-health. This book is designed to help people who are interested in their diet to know what they are eating and to enable them to make informed choices within nutritional guidelines.

In Chapter 1 we look at what is meant by a 'healthy' diet. This is now seen to be very important for the promotion of health and well-being. The fact that diet is a recognized risk factor in the development of certain diseases common in our society is highly topical and we look into this further. Guidelines for changing your diet to make it more health-promoting are given.

To understand the link between diet and health we need to know what is in our food and what we need to get from it. This is dealt with in Chapter 2 where nutrients are discussed with special reference to food sources, functions and how to prevent nutrient losses.

It is interesting to know how much we need of the various nutrients and this somewhat controversial issue is what Chapter 3 is all about. A large summary table for recommended daily amounts of nutrients is given. However, despite the focus on figures in this chapter we come back to foods again and explain how a healthy mixture of food can be achieved. This is important because 'we eat foods, not nutrients'.

The health-food trade is, without doubt, big business in Britain, though it is not altogether clear what a health food is. Nevertheless, there are health-food shops in almost every high street and most supermarkets carry foods that were not seen outside specialist shops as recently as five years ago. Chapter 4 is about health foods – what they are and what they do. A general insight into the use of food additives is also given.

If you are concerned about the use of food additives you will undoubtedly be used to looking at food labels! Chapter 5 is about the minefield of food labelling. The main theme of the chapter is to show you how to interpret the information presented on food labels so that you can assess the nutritional quality of food.

To make our guide to healthy eating fully comprehensive Chapter 6 is about different types of diet, for there is no such thing as a single healthy diet. These include diets for groups with special needs such as pregnant women, children and the elderly, and diets which are followed for social, religious or ethical reasons, e.g. vegetarian, macrobiotic, Rastafarian. Some of these diets need special attention to ensure nutritional sufficiency and some, for example, the vegetarian diet, are good examples of a healthy diet. Diet also has a part to play in the treatment of some diseases. We briefly discuss some of the more common diets that are used and a very general guide to feeding the convalescent is given.

To make our guide to healthy eating complete Chapters 7 and 8 tell you how to judge if your diet is healthy and what to do about it if it is not. Chapter 8 is largely taken up with tables which give the nutritional value of food portions so you can see at a glance what is in the food you are eating. For you to assess if your diet is 'healthy' you need to know what nutrients are in the food you are eating. The tables are your instant ready reckoner for this information. The nutritional value of around 600 food portions is included.

Chapter 1

Diet and Health: The Link

The old adage says that 'we are what we eat'. This is true since the components of our bodies and the energy and nutrients required to make them work efficiently come from our food. It is not surprising that if our diet doesn't supply what we need our bodies will not work efficiently and we are likely to become ill.

We hear foods referred to as 'healthy' or 'unhealthy'. However, we do not eat single foods but a mixture of foods which together compose our diet. If a diet consists of a single food, no matter what that food is, it will be 'unhealthy' because no single food can contribute all the nutrients we require in the right proportions. This is, perhaps, another way of saying that we can have too much of a good thing! From a nutritional standpoint it is doubtful if any food can be said to be 'unhealthy'. It depends upon the amount of it we eat in relation to the diet as a whole. There is a popular notion that some foods are 'junk' because they contribute nothing, or practically nothing, but sugar to the diet. If these foods contribute a major proportion of our total energy then there may well be cause for concern. But they cannot be simply dismissed as 'junk'. After all, sugar is a source of energy!

In the last ten to fifteen years there has been a considerable change in systems of food distribution. The once familiar grocer's shop has largely disappeared and been replaced by the supermarket and hypermarket. Shopping in bulk at relatively infrequent intervals is now the rule rather than the exception. Some people have little time available or time that they are willing to spend on food preparation. This has resulted in an increasing demand for 'convenience' foods. These are foods that require the minimum of preparation in the home and very often only a final cooking before serving. The rapid growth in the convenience food market has involved an increasing use of canning and freezing as a means of food preservation and a tremendous increase in the ownership of home freezers.

For some people, the increasing use of convenience foods has given cause for concern about nutritional quality. Research has, however, shown that the nutritional differences between preserved and fresh fruit and vegetables are less than the differences likely to occur in fresh fruit and vegetables under normal conditions. This is particularly true of vitamin C.

Changing social conditions have also led, among other things, to a substantial decrease in family meals. Not only has there been an increasing reliance on convenience foods, but also a tremendous increase in the availability of 'fast' foods. These are foods that are ready to eat when purchased. Fish and chips are possibly the most familiar fast foods in the UK but the range has been greatly expanded by the McDonald's, Kentucky Fried Chicken and other chains. Most of the foods sold through these outlets contain an undesirable amount of saturated fat and only very small amounts of some vitamins such as folic acid. Clearly, if fast foods form the major part of your food intake you will have an unhealthy diet. However, there is no reason why you shouldn't eat these foods occasionally. It is the diet with which we are concerned rather than with 'healthy' or 'unhealthy' foods.

A balanced diet?

The idea of a balanced diet stems from the recognition that mixes of different food items will provide the minimum amounts of energy, protein, minerals and vitamins that are required by your body to maintain health. Nutrients lacking in one food will be 'balanced' or made up by the larger amounts provided by other foods. Thus, the greater the variety of foods in your diet the more likely it will be for the supply of energy or any nutrient to be adequate. The emphasis behind the term 'balanced diet' was the prevention of nutrient deficiencies and it has been recommended by the National Advisory Committee on Nutrition Education (NACNE) that we should now think rather more positively about our diet, putting the emphasis on health rather than disease. The Committee suggested that this idea and also the need for variety would be expressed in the term 'healthy varied diet'.

A healthy varied diet?

To ensure that your diet is healthy and varied it is important that you eat a sound mixture of foods. To do this it is convenient to think about foods in groups on the basis of their nutritional attributes. Generally, food grouping is a controversial issue in the field of nutrition. However, the scheme presented here will enable you to arrive at a 'healthy varied diet'. Plan your meals to include representation of cereals, preferably unrefined, vegetables or fruit and some or any one of the following: meat, fish, eggs, milk, yogurt, cheese, pulses, nuts. You may choose other foods such as sugar, fat and salt but try to eat these in moderation. For full details of our meal-planning scheme see Chapter 7 (p.85).

A healthy varied diet – whose responsibility?

The food we eat is for most of us a matter of personal choice within the limits of our purse. It is therefore possible for us to take responsibility to try to keep healthy. But if we are to choose food wisely to create a healthy diet a knowledge of food composition is important. However, this is not only a personal matter, since catering officers, chefs and indeed anyone who provides meals should realize that their choice of food, recipes and cooking methods can play an important part in helping to prevent disease and promote health. The Government and other agencies have given a lead in this matter through the publication of dietary goals. A summary of these goals is given in Table 1.1.

Table 1.1 Summary of dietary goals

Source	Dietary recommendations
NACNE (1983)	*Obesity* Adjust types of food eaten and increase exercise output to maintain optimal limits of weight for height.
	Fat Reduce fat to 30% energy intake.
	Saturated fat Reduce saturated fat to 10% energy intake.
	Sugar Reduce sugar intake to 10kg per head per year.
	Fibre Increase fibre to 30g per head per day.
	Salt Reduce salt intake by 3g per head per day.
	Alcohol Reduce alcohol to 4% energy intake.
	Protein Eat more vegetable protein at the expense of animal protein.
COMA (1984)	*Obesity* Adjust food intake in relation to physical activity until weight is within the acceptable range.
	Fat Reduce fat to 35% energy intake.
	Saturated fat Reduce saturated fat to 15% energy intake.
	Sugar No further increase in sugar intake.
	Fibre Compensate for reduced fat with increased fibre-rich carbohydrates.
	Salt No further increase in salt intake.
	Alcohol Excess alcohol to be avoided.
	Protein No specific recommendation.

Source	Dietary recommendations
JACNE (1985)	*Obesity* A lower fat diet combined with moderate regular exercise is a healthy way to slim. *Fat* Eat less fat. *Saturated fat* Eat less saturated fat. *Sugar* Go easy on sugar. *Fibre* Increase fruit and vegetables. *Salt* Go easy on salt. *Alcohol* Go easy on alcohol. *Protein* No specific recommendation.

(Taken from Davies J and Hammond B, 'Cooking Explained' 3rd Edition, Longman 1988)
NACNE – National Advisory Committee on Nutrition Education, 'Proposals for nutritional guidelines for health education in Britain', Health Education Council (1983).
COMA – Committee on Medical Aspects of Food Policy, 'Diet and cardiovascular disease', Her Majesty's Stationery Office (1984).
JACNE – The British Nutrition Foundation and Health Education Council Joint Advisory Committee on Nutrition Education, 'Eating for a healthier heart', Health Education Council (1985).

Diet and health

The importance of dietary goals stems from the relationship between diet and certain diseases. Some of the major health disorders prevalent in Britain have a strong association with food. This will become clear as we discuss some of the more common disorders.

Obesity is considered to be the most common nutritional disorder in Britain today. If you are 20 per cent or more above your desirable weight for height you are said to be obese. The cause of obesity is simple – the individual is consuming more energy than is required. However, this explanation often hides the complexity of the condition, for there may be psychological reasons for the excess energy consumption, and metabolic reasons why, for some, even with an intake considerably below expected requirements, it is difficult to lose weight. Many people who are not obese may feel that they are overweight and wish to lose weight for aesthetic rather than health reasons. There is no good evidence that a moderate degree of overweight is harmful, but obesity is associated with a number of disorders including coronary heart disease, diabetes, gallstones, gout, osteoarthritis, cancer, respiratory disorders and varicose veins.

For most of us it is not an excessive food intake that results in weight gain but the consumption of just a little more than is needed over a long time. There are complex body mechanisms that control food intake but in humans these mechanisms are often overridden by higher centres in the brain. We do not usually eat because we are hungry but because it is customary to eat at certain times, because of social pressures or even in the course of business.

Clearly, if you know you are putting on weight you need to change your diet to reduce your energy intake. Examine the energy values of food in Chapter 8 to enable you to do this. Try to increase the fibre content of your diet because this may act as an obstacle to energy intake. Fibre is bulky and also results in a greater loss of energy in the faeces. As well as this pay attention to meal spacing. Try to have three meals a day to ensure an equal distribution of energy throughout the day. The large meal at the end of the day with little food throughout the day is often a recipe for obesity.

Dental caries is widespread in Britain. There is considerable evidence that dental caries is linked with the consumption of sugar. However, the link is not a simple one for the effects of sucrose can be reduced by the fluoridation of drinking water, toothpastes and mouthwashes and by scrupulous dental hygiene. The high incidence of dental caries in very young children in parts of London is associated with prolonged irrigation of the teeth with sugar-rich drinks. The erosion of teeth involves the removal of minerals from tooth enamel by acid. This is produced by the action of bacterial enzymes on certain carbohydrates, e.g. sugary and fibre-depleted foods such as white bread.

To reduce your chances of having rotten teeth there are some very positive things you can do. Avoid eating sugary foods and soft, fibre-depleted foods between meals as these foods have a tendency to stick to the teeth. Go for high-fibre foods. These require more chewing and consequently are more easily cleared from the mouth. Ensure that your intake of fluoride is adequate. The main source of this is water. Note that seafish and tea, particularly China tea, are useful sources of fluoride.

Coronary heart disease (CHD) is the commonest cause of death in men aged thirty-five to fifty-five years in the UK. A number of factors contribute to a person's risk of developing CHD. Prevention involves the adoption of a pattern of healthy living which includes modification of diet. Coronary heart disease includes:

- angina pectoris – serious chest pains
- myocardial infarction – heart attack
- sudden death

Cerebrovascular disease, often just referrred to as a 'stroke', may cause disabilities such as loss of speech, paralysis of limbs and, in severe cases, sudden death. Women tend to be more prone to strokes than men.

Both coronary heart disease and strokes result from severe atherosclerosis. This is the deposition of a complex of fatty substances on the inner walls of the arteries which reduces the size of the tube through which the blood flows. This is shown in Figure 1.1.

The level of cholesterol in the blood is a major factor in causing atherosclerosis. The blood cholesterol level is increased by a high level of fat, and particularly of saturated fat, in the diet. Fat which contains polyunsaturated fatty acids, such as sunflower seed oil, is

Figure 1.1 Atherosclerosis

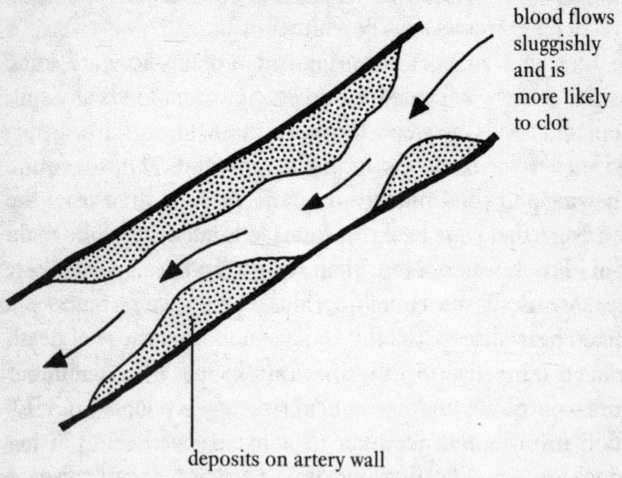

much less dangerous and may, in fact, reduce the blood cholesterol level.

For a long time it seemed difficult to explain why Eskimos with their high-fat diet had a low death rate from CHD. We now believe that this is because the fatty fish that they eat contain a particular fatty acid which makes blood clot much less readily. It may be sensible to eat more fatty fish such as herring and mackerel.

Hypertension (high blood pressure) is a recognized risk factor for CHD and there is evidence that a high intake of salt may, in some people, contribute to this disorder.

High intakes of dietary fibre are associated with a reduction in the incidence of CHD. This could be because a high-fibre diet helps to reduce energy intake. People who are overweight are more likely to develop hypertension and to have higher blood levels of cholesterol. Fibre may act in another way, for example, refined carbohydrate causes a rapid rise in blood insulin levels and excessive amounts of insulin increase the likelihood of developing atherosclerosis.

The UK has been described as a 'constipated nation', but the condition is less common in vegetarians (non-meat eaters) and vegans (eat plant foods only) than in omnivores. The diagnosis of constipation is not easy. However, the condition is associated with infrequent defaecation and the passage of small, hard stools. Straining is necessary to empty the bowel. Though constipation can have other causes, it is often prevented by a high-fibre, and particularly high-cereal fibre intake. The prevention of constipation is not only important for its own sake but also because it may contribute to other diseases including hiatus hernia, haemorrhoids, diverticular disease, appendicitis, cancer of the large bowel and varicose veins.

Obviously an important part of healthy eating is the avoidance of food poisoning. Bacteria are the main culprits, including Salmonella, Listeria monocytogenes, Staphylococcus aureus, Clostridium perfringens, Clostridium botulinum and Bacillus cereus. It is important to pay attention to sensible shopping, storage, thawing frozen food, cooking and reheating foods, kitchen and personal hygiene. For more details on this see Further Reading on p.122.

Dietary change

By now you should be convinced that diet and health are closely linked. The dietary risk factors associated with the particular disorders discussed give full support to the dietary goals that are summarized in Table 1.1. However, dietary goals are perhaps a little abstract and they need to be translated into the food that we eat. Putting dietary goals into practice is not as difficult as it might at first seem. There are very positive things you can do. General pointers for this are given in Chapter 7 (p.70). Our tables of food composition in Chapter 8 will enable you to see how you can modify your diet without too much difficulty.

Be patient and remember that eating habits do not change overnight. Allow yourself plenty of time to adjust.

Chapter 2

What is in our Food?

The fact that 'we are what we eat' means that food must supply the energy that we need for life, and a range of body constituents needed to perform various functions in our tissues. Proteins supply amino acids for the building of body proteins, including enzymes. A variety of vitamins are required in very small quantities to work with the enzymes to drive the various metabolic processes. In addition, different minerals are needed for health. One of these, calcium, is required to make our skeletons strong, whilst smaller amounts of others are needed to control our body fluids and still others to work with the vitamins and enzymes in metabolism.

Energy

The body cannot function without a supply of energy. When at rest, not doing any physical work in a comfortably warm environment, we need energy to keep the internal organs ticking over and to maintain our body temperature. This energy is called the 'basal' or 'resting' energy level.

We need more energy when our physical activity increases. Some examples of the energy needed for a variety of physical activities is shown in Table 2.1. Energy expenditure when resting and during various activities differs considerably in different people. But as a general rule, the amount of energy required for a particular activity tends to be reduced by training and experience.

Table 2.1 Energy expenditure for a range of physical activities

kcal per hour	Activity
100	Housework
130–240	Walking
200–700	Swimming
600–1000	Running

On the other hand, the rate at which the activity is pursued increases the energy expenditure.

If you take in more energy than you need this leads to an increase in body fat. But the amount of energy required to maintain a constant body weight may vary as much as fourfold, from one individual to another. People with high energy intakes are not necessarily fat and those with low energy intakes are not always slim.

Energy is derived from the oxidation of carbohydrate, fat and protein. If the energy intake is not sufficient to meet the body's needs for energy, body tissues will be broken down. This is, of course, the basis of slimming diets in which it is hoped that people will lose fat but retain lean body tissue. The energy content of a diet can be roughly calculated from a knowledge of its carbohydrate, fat and protein content assuming that 1 gram of each will produce 4, 9 and 4 kcal respectively. The other source of energy in the diet is alcohol which yields 7 kcal per gram. It is not too surprising that alcoholics have a poor appetite!

High-protein foods tend to be more expensive than those containing large amounts of starch. It is therefore good dietary practice to 'spare' proteins, to reduce their likelihood of being used as a source of energy, by eating some starchy foods with high-protein foods. Thus, fish and chips and roast beef and Yorkshire pudding are not only good foods, they also make sound dietary sense. Increasing the consumption of foods that are rich in starch fits in with dietary goals.

Carbohydrate

The contribution of carbohydrates to the energy content of the human diet may be as low as 40 per cent in rich countries and as high as 85 per cent in poor ones. The desirable level is 60–65 per cent. Carbohydrates are manufactured by plants using carbon dioxide, water and sunlight. There are different types of plant carbohydrate. One is known collectively as fibre or roughage. This component of our food was for a long time ignored but has now been recognized as being very important for health. We have already mentioned it in the section on 'Dietary goals' and in connection with a number of diseases. The average diet in the UK contains about 20g per day of fibre. It has been suggested that this should be increased to 25–30g per day. You can easily increase the fibre content of your diet by following the guidelines in Chapter 7.

Other types of carbohydrate are the simple sugars, of which sucrose is the most important, and the complex starches which are composed of glucose units. The only carbohydrate obtained from animals in any quantity is lactose contained in milk. Simple sugars are absorbed rapidly into the bloodstream whereas the digestion of starch takes longer. This, together with their occurrence with fibre, makes a high intake of starches desirable.

There is limited storage of carbohydrate as glycogen in the liver and muscles. Normally this store does not amount to more than about 350g in an adult. Diets for some kinds of sportsmen and athletes are designed to maximize the glycogen stores.

The ability to utilize lactose is greatest in babies. It persists in Caucasian adults but is limited in non-Caucasians due to loss of the enzyme lactase in the gut. This enzyme is necessary for the digestion of lactose. Only small amounts of milk can be tolerated by non-Caucasians.

Proteins

Proteins consist of long chains of amino acids – substances which contain nitrogen. There are 22 different types of amino acid present in the proteins of the human body. In adults eight, and, in young children, ten, of these are described as 'essential'. This means that it is essential to provide them in the diet because the body cannot make them. Formerly where the essential amino acids were present in adequate quantities in food proteins they used to be described as 'first class proteins'; otherwise they were 'second class'. The former were on the whole derived from animals, the latter from plants. This distinction is now no longer made because we recognize that individual proteins are not usually eaten – we eat a mixture of foods providing a mixture of proteins. Even if meat and all foods of animal origin are excluded from the diet, as in a 'vegan diet', it is still possible to obtain adequate amounts of all the essential amino acids from a mixture of plant proteins – the proteins of one food complementing those of another.

Proteins are broken down in the gut to their composite units and the amino acids are then absorbed. Amino acids are needed to make body proteins in the processes of growth and repair, and also to make enzymes and certain hormones, called 'peptide' hormones. Proteins are made at a much faster rate in babies and young children than in young adults and faster in young adults compared with old people. The difference between the intake of protein nitrogen and the excretion of nitrogen from the body in urine and faeces is known as the 'nitrogen balance'. When growth or the repair of body tissue is occurring more nitrogen is retained and the balance is positive. Normally adults are 'in balance' whereas in individuals who are breaking down their body proteins, the balance is negative. Breakdown of body proteins occurs when it is necessary to use their constituent amino acids as a source of energy.

Because of their requirements for growth, children need more protein of better quality than do adults.

The protein content of foods is variable. Some foods, for example, meat, fish, eggs and pulses are particularly protein rich. However, the quantity of protein in a food may be misleading in judging its value for growth or the maintenance of tissue. The quality of a protein depends on its amino acid content. But proteins can be mixed to complement each other so that the amino acid content of the diet is adequate. For example, it is important to eat pulses with cereals: hummus and pitta bread; beans on toast; dahl with rice. These food combinations ensure a good quality protein.

The body cannot store protein in the sense that it can store energy as fat. If too little protein or too little energy is taken in the diet, tissue protein, and particularly muscle protein, will be broken down. If more protein is eaten than is necessary to meet our requirements then the amino acids will be broken down. The nitrogen from them is excreted in the urine and the remainder of the protein converted into body fat.

Fats

Fat is the body's main store of energy and dietary fats are the most concentrated source of energy. The fats in animal tissues are mainly saturated and are solid at room temperature. Too much saturated fat is now thought to be bad for you and it is particularly saturated fat which tends to lead to an increase in blood cholesterol levels. The unsaturated fats of plants and fish oils on the other hand, whilst still having the same energy value, tend to reduce blood cholesterol levels. Unsaturated fats have lower melting points and vegetable and fish oils are rich in polyunsaturated fatty acids including those that are described as 'essential fatty acids' or EFAs. These are necessary for the maintenance of cell membranes and for the compounds called prostaglandins which protect us against cardiovascular disease. The amount and nature of dietary fat is a keystone for a healthy diet.

Vitamins

Vitamins are substances needed by the body in small amounts which mostly function with enzymes and which the body cannot make, at least in sufficient quantities to meet requirements. They are divided into two groups – water-soluble (B group and C) and fat-soluble (A, D, E and K). The former are not stored in the body in appreciable quantities and are much less toxic than the latter. Most of the common vitamins have been known by letters of the alphabet and these letters will be used here where possible because of their common usage. There is more popular interest in vitamins than in any other group of nutrients. Since many of them are easily obtainable in large quantities over the counter it is understandable that panacea-like properties have been attributed to them. Alas, many people are lured into spending quite large amounts of money in searching for these properties. We suggest that often the effects are psychological rather than biological.

Vitamin B_1 (thiamine) Vitamin B_1 is needed to help us to derive energy from carbohydrate. It is not surprising therefore that the amount needed is related to energy intake. Severe deficiency of vitamin B_1 causes a disease called beri-beri, which is due to the effect on the function of the heart. B_1 deficiency also affects the function of the nervous system. Its effect on peripheral nerves is shown by tingling, pins and needles, numbness and foot 'drop'. Beri-beri is characteristic of rice-eating countries. During the polishing of rice, vitamin B_1 is removed in the husk.

In the UK, B_1 deficiency is principally found amongst chronic alcoholics and old people. In both groups it is due to a poor diet. In chronic alcoholics a condition develops which resembles beri-beri, and some alcoholics sustain permanent damage to the brain. Vitamin B_1 deficiency is, however, far more common in old people, in whom it can cause mental confusion and heart disease.

Vitamin B_1 is present in a number of plant foods and in dairy produce (excluding butter), but we obtain a large amount from cereals. As with rice, a large amount of the vitamin is removed in the husk during milling but it is one of the vitamins added back by law to white flour. It is also added to many breakfast cereals. Some meats, particularly pork, are useful sources.

Because thiamine is water-soluble, the water used for cooking vegetables will contain a substantial amount of the vitamin and should always be used for making gravy. The vitamin is quickly destroyed in alkaline solutions and baking powder should never be used with vegetables. As a rough guide it can be assumed that 25 per cent of vitamin B_1 will be lost in cooking a mixed diet. Normal methods of food preservation result in only small losses.

It is recommended that our diet should contain 0.4mg vitamin B_1/1000 kcal, i.e. about 1mg per day for most people.

Vitamin B_2 (riboflavin) Like thiamine and nicotinic acid riboflavin is needed to help us derive energy from carbohydrate. Deficiency of riboflavin is not common but it may occur as part of a multiple deficiency of B vitamins. The usual signs of deficiency include cracked and sore lips. The tongue becomes sore and magenta in colour.

Major food sources of riboflavin include milk, cheese, eggs, meat, offal, and yeast extract.

Riboflavin is less water soluble and more stable to heat than thiamine but it is sensitive to light. Milk left on the doorstep loses the vitamin because is is destroyed by ultraviolet light.

The recommended intake of riboflavin is 1.4mg per day for women and 1.6mg per day for men.

Vitamin B_3 (nicotinic acid, niacin) Deficiency of vitamin B_3 is associated with a disease, pellagra, which affects the skin, the gastrointestinal tract and the brain. Pellagra is found in countries where maize is the staple food. Much of the vitamin B_3 in this cereal is in a bound form and only after treatment with alkali does it become available in the human body. Skin changes similar to those found in pellagra are sometimes seen in old people. The skin lesions have a particular distribution like socks, gloves and a necklace.

Nicotinic acid is widely distributed in both plant and animal foods but only in small amounts. The richest sources are meat, (especially liver), fish, wholemeal cereals (it is added to white flour) and pulses.

Cooking itself causes little destruction of nicotinic acid but losses from meat occur in the 'drippings'.

The recommended intake is 6.6mg per 1000 kcal.

Vitamin B_6 (pyridoxine) Disease due to vitamin B_6 deficiency is unknown in adults. Some drugs, such as isoniazid, used for the treatment of tuberculosis, and oestrogens and oral contraceptives increase the requirement for vitamin B_6. Vitamin B_6 plays an important role in the activity of many enzymes involved in the metabolism of amino acids and proteins.

This vitamin is found in many foods – cereals, meats, fruits and leafy and other vegetables. No foods contain large amounts, but most adult diets contain 1.5–2.0mg which is the recommended intake.

Large doses, up to 600mg/day of vitamin B_6 have been prescribed for the treatment of premenstrual syndrome (PMS) but doses of 50mg or more per day can be toxic.

Vitamin B_{12} (cyanocobalamin) and folic acid These are often called the 'anaemia-preventing vitamins' since they are both involved in the formation of red blood cells. Deficiency of either vitamin causes an anaemia in which the number of red cells is reduced but their size is increased. Folic acid will cure anaemia due to vitamin B_{12} deficiency but it is very important to detect B_{12} deficiency because this vitamin is also important for the function of the central nervous system. Simply curing the anaemia could leave the person with permanent damage to the brain and spinal cord. Vitamin B_{12} is absorbed in a very special way because it needs to be linked to a substance called the 'intrinsic factor' which is formed in the stomach. This means that deficiency of the vitamin can occur due to a failure to produce intrinsic factor or because of a dietary deficiency of the vitamin. The former occurs in persons who have had operations on the stomach, and in persons who have the disease called pernicious anaemia. Dietary deficiency occurs in people who do not consume foods of animal origin because these are the only usual dietary source. (See p.37 for sources of B_{12} for non-meat eaters.) Liver is the richest source of B_{12} and we need only a very small amount, 2μg per day.

Folic acid exists in foodstuffs in a form which has to be broken down by enzymes in the intestine. The food values for folic acid are not very accurate, due to unsatisfactory analytical methods.

The richest sources of folic acid are liver and green vegetables. There is some uncertainty in the UK about the recommended allowance, but 200μg seems to be a reasonable estimate. Folic acid deficiency in pregnant women may be a cause of fetal malformations, particularly spina bifida.

Vitamin C (ascorbic acid) This vitamin is needed for the formation of connective tissue, the packaging material that separates, protects and supports organs in the body. There is a large amount of connective tissue in the skin and it is here that signs of deficiency are seen in the disease, scurvy. The skin bruises easily, cuts take a long time to heal and gums start to bleed. Vitamin C performs many other functions in the body and some of these functions may be interfered with before there are signs of scurvy. In this country scurvy is rare but it does occur in old people and particularly in widowers living alone.

Vitamin C aids the absorption of inorganic iron. It is advisable always to take extra vitamin C if you are taking an iron supplement.

In the UK the most important source of vitamin C for many people is potatoes. This is not because they are a rich source but because we normally eat a reasonable amount of them every day. New potatoes contain more vitamin C than old ones. Green vegetables and citrus fruits are good sources but the amount in vegetables depends on how they have been cooked. The amount of water and the cooking time must be kept to a minimum. They should also be eaten as soon as possible after cooking. Keeping vegetables hot quickly destroys the vitamin. It must also be remembered that vitamin C is soluble in water and if vegetables are left soaking for a long time some of the vitamin will be leached out. Interestingly, chips retain vitamin C because it is 'sealed' into the chips by the fat. Vitamin C is added to some fruit drinks and these then become good sources of the vitamin. A large amount of vitamin C is used in food processing so there may be 'hidden' sources of the vitamin. This probably accounts for the fact that some people may apparently have very low intakes but have no sign of deficiency.

The UK recommended intake is 30mg per day which is the amount in one good-sized orange. Larger amounts are recommended by authorities in other countries who use different criteria on which to base their recommendations. It is probable that the UK value is too low. In fact, the results of more recent research suggest that the value should be nearer 80mg per day. Women seem to need more than men and smoking considerably increases the requirement.

Many people are encouraged to take 'mega', that is gram quantities of vitamin C because of popularized suggestions that it will prevent the common cold and certain sorts of cancer. There is no good evidence to support these suggestions. Severe illness, major surgery and infections do increase requirements and supplements of say, 200mg per day, are certainly advisable for the sick.

Vitamin A (retinol) Deficiency of this vitamin is a major cause of blindness in the world because of its effects on the cornea and conjunctiva. Deficiency also causes night-blindness because the vitamin is an important constituent of the pigment, visual purple, which is present in the retina. Currently, there is considerable interest in the possibility that deficiency of vitamin A may predispose persons to develop certain types of cancer. However, it seems likely that this protective function is not due to retinol but to the carotene in our foods which can be converted into vitamin A. Beta-carotene has properties that are distinct from vitamin A. In particular its protective role against cancer may be due to its antioxidant properties.

We obtain preformed vitamin A from foods of animal origin. Liver is a particularly good source because the vitamin is stored there. Polar bear liver contains so much vitamin A that a very small amount is toxic. Beta-carotene is found in all coloured vegetables. Both retinol and carotene are stable in ordinary cooking methods. Because we derive vitamin A from two sources dietary vitamin A is quoted as retinol equivalents. The recommended intake for adults in the UK is 750μg retinol equivalents per day.

Over-zealous consumption of vitamin A should be avoided and in particular the taking of vitamin A supplements. These have been given by doctors for the treatment of acne. They should be particularly avoided by women during pregnancy as they can result in fetal malformations.

Vitamin D (cholecalciferol) This substance is a vitamin, that is a dietary essential, only for those people who are not exposed to sufficient ultraviolet light to make it in their skin. For those of us who do not have a dietary requirement, cholecalciferol is more correctly considered to be a hormone. Deficiency of vitamin D causes rickets in children and osteomalacia in adults. Bow legs, swollen knees (knocked knees), swollen wrists and swollen ends of ribs ('rachitic rosary') are characteristic signs of rickets in children and result from derangement of bone formation at the growing ends. In the UK this disease is almost always limited to Asian children.

Osteomalacia, in which bone fails to mineralize, is characterized by bone weakness and increased proneness to fractures. This also is found in Asians. In both adults and young Asians the skin is often covered and the sunlight not strong enough to penetrate the dark skin. Osteomalacia is also found among white old people in the UK and again is primarily due to lack of exposure of the skin to UV light. If the skin is exposed during the summer there is a good chance of making sufficient cholecalciferol to last through the winter. In old people, osteomalacia is a common deficiency disease and along with senile osteoporosis, or thinning of the bones, is a major cause of hip fractures.

Only a few foods are rich sources of vitamin D. These include fish (herring and mackerel), canned sardines and pilchards, eggs, butter, cheese and cream. It is added by law to margarine and this is, therefore, a much more reliable source than butter in which the amount of vitamin D is lower in winter than in summer. In the UK there is no recommended dietary allowance for adults as it is assumed that they will make sufficient in their skin. The recommended allowance for children is 10μg and for old people 2.5μg.

This vitamin, like vitamin A, being fat-soluble is toxic. Too much causes raised calcium level in blood, headache, depression and irritability. Young children are sometimes given cod liver oil as a source of vitamin D. Too much can be fatal.

Vitamin E (tocopherols) The only known deficiency occurs in premature babies and shows itself as a haemolytic anaemia.

The richest sources are vegetable oils of which wheatgerm is the best. The US recommended dietary intake is 10mg for men but people who are taking a considerable amount of polyunsaturates will need more. However, since it occurs in the foods that are rich sources of polyunsaturates it is probable that special provision of vitamin E is not necessary.

This is another vitamin whose consumption in quantities much greater than the recommended level has been encouraged. Many people are taking wheatgerm capsules and amounts of vitamin E up to 300mg or more per day. Generally speaking, these supplements are being taken in an attempt to slow down the ageing process and also to help to prevent cardiovascular disease. These vitamin E supplements are unlikely to do any harm unless warfarin is being taken as a drug to help to prevent a clot forming in the circulation. In such people large amounts of vitamin E may cause a spontaneous haemorrhage. Whether the supplements will have a beneficial effect is not at present known.

Vitamin K (naphthoquinones) The only known function for these substances is in the series of events which leads to the clotting of blood. Deficiency may occur in infants but is very rare in adults. The vitamin is present in fresh green leafy vegetables such as lettuce, broccoli, cabbage and spinach. Ox liver is also a good source.

Minerals

The main deposit of minerals is in the bones which owe their rigidity and hardness to the presence of a mineral deposit which is a mixture of calcium phosphate and calcium hydroxide. Some minerals, zinc for example, work with, or are constituents of important enzymes. Minerals present in foods originate from the soil. The total amount of a particular mineral in the diet may be a poor indicator of the amount that is available to the body. All the mineral may not be liberated from the food as it passes down the digestive tract. Furthermore, minerals may react with each other or with substances in the digestive tract and in this way may also be made unavailable. Generally, minerals that are present in foods of animal origin are better absorbed than those in plants.

Calcium The adult human body contains about 1200g of calcium. All but about 0.5 per cent of this is in the bones and teeth, largely in association with a connective tissue protein, collagen. The small amount of calcium outside the skeleton has very important functions. The calcium in the blood is essential for blood clotting and for the activity of muscles and nerves. When the blood level falls below a certain critical level the muscles in the hand contract, a condition known as 'tetany'.

Vitamin D is essential for the absorption of calcium from the gut.

Animals are able to concentrate calcium in milk and milk products are the main dietary source of the mineral. Calcium in vegetables is absorbed to a varying degree as, too, is the calcium of whole cereals. Calcium carbonate is added to white flour so this, too, becomes a good source. Meats are a poor source of calcium.

In the UK the recommended daily amount for calcium is presently 500mg, but many think that this is not enough. There is increasing evidence to suggest that an intake of 1000mg per day is desirable in order to reduce the risk of osteoporosis as we get older. Bones that contain more mineral at maturity are more resistant to bone loss in old age. More calcium is needed during pregnancy and lactation. A mother who is breast feeding her baby will lose about 250mg of calcium in her milk daily.

Iron The human body contains about 4g of iron. The mineral is stored in the liver and to some extent in the kidneys. In the blood it is present in the red pigment, haemoglobin, which carries oxygen from the lungs to the tissues. In the muscles there is a similar iron-containing substance called myoglobin. In the tissues it is present in compounds which play an important role in the oxidation of many substances. The body cannot excrete iron so that the iron released when red cells are destroyed is stored in the liver. This happens when a person has had blood transfusions. All the iron in the blood given to them remains in their body.

Meat, meat products, cereals, vegetables and fruits all contain iron but amounts vary greatly in different samples. Iron is more easily absorbed when it is derived from foods of animal origin. It is advisable to take vitamin C with iron preparations (see p.18). Normally, we absorb only about 10 per cent of the dietary iron. Persons who are anaemic will absorb a greater proportion.

Iron deficiency causes anaemia. This condition can be caused by dietary deficiency or by blood losses, as for example, due to menstruation. The recommended daily amount for adult men is 10mg and for women 12mg. Women need more iron than men because during menstruation they lose about 25mg of iron. Larger amounts are required during pregnancy and lactation, although milk is generally a poor source of iron. The iron in human milk is more easily absorbed than that in cow's milk.

Zinc The adult human body contains about 2g of this mineral or about half the amount of iron. Zinc is a constituent of over 70 enzymes. High concentrations are found in parts of the eye, and in men, in the prostate. High concentrations are also found in the skin and bones.

Zinc deficiency causes a rare congenital disorder, and may also occur in severely malnourished children and adults. There is no UK recommended daily amount for zinc and it is customary to use the American one of 15mg per day. Although most British diets contain less than this, there is no evidence that zinc deficiency occurs in healthy persons living on any of the diets commonly consumed in this country. Good dietary sources are meats, whole grains and legumes. The richest food source is oysters. Like calcium, zinc binds to phytate and other components of dietary fibre and this reduces the amount absorbed. However, there is no evidence that this reduced absorption can cause zinc depletion in western countries. It could do so in poor countries where a large amount of energy comes from unrefined carbohydrates and also in food faddists who overdose themselves with bran.

Iodine Iodine, which is found in the thyroid gland, is a constituent of thyroxine, the hormone which regulates the metabolic rate. Iodine deficiency causes the thyroid gland to enlarge, a condition known as 'goitre'. This occurs in areas where the iodine content of food and water is low and also in areas where vegetables are consumed which contain substances known as 'goitrogens'. Vegetables belonging to the Brassica family (cabbage, etc.) contain goitrogens but they are not an important cause of goitre in the UK. Millet, a staple food in parts of Africa, also contains goitrogens and these are a health hazard.

The iodine content of food depends on the amount in the environment in which the food is grown. Most soils are poor in iodine so most foods are poor sources. The richest source is seafood. Fish contain variable amounts but they are generally richer sources than fruit, vegetables, meat and meat products. Iodine is added to table salt in some countries as a preventive measure.

Fluorine The main interest in this mineral is in its anti-caries property. At a concentration of 1 part per million (ppm) in drinking water it affords significant protection against tooth decay. At higher concentrations it causes brown spots, or mottling, to appear on the teeth. Large intakes are poisonous and cause thickening and increased calcification of the bones. Protection of teeth against decay results from the formation in the teeth of a particular kind of mineral, fluorapatite, which is more resistant to attack by oral acids.

Apart from drinking water to which fluoride may be added as a prophylactic, public health measure, tea is a significant source. Many toothpastes also contain fluoride.

Selenium Much has been written about this trace element in recent years. It is irregularly distributed in soils, so in some parts of the world plants may contain too much and this causes diseases in livestock grazing on them. In other parts, notably New Zealand and parts of China, the soils contain too little. In China selenium deficiency causes a severe form of heart disease, or cardiomyopathy, known as Keshan disease, which can be prevented with sodium selenite. Selenium is an integral part of an enzyme which protects fats against oxidative damage. Selenium thus has properties that are similar to those of vitamin E.

Most of our selenium comes from cereals and meat.

Other minerals Besides these minerals a number of trace elements – manganese, molybdenum, chromium, cobalt, silicon, vanadium and nickel – have been considered essential nutrients for animals and, by inference, for man. Phosphorus is associated with calcium in bones and teeth and as part of various organic constituents in the soft tissue but deficiency is very unlikely to occur in man. Magnesium is also found in the skeleton and as a part of many enzymes in the cells. However, magnesium deficiency is unknown in disease-free humans. The electrolytes, sodium and potassium are also, of course, derived from the diet. Sodium deficiency cannot be produced solely by reducing the salt content of the diet. The kidney is very efficient in conserving salt and it is only when losses occur as a result of sweating that deficiency occurs causing severe cramps. This condition is prevented, or treated, with sodium chloride tablets. For some people excessive consumption of salt is linked with high blood pressure.

Potassium deficiency has been found to occur in some old people in whom it was associated with mental confusion and muscle weakness.

Water

Water is often forgotten in a consideration of nutrients. Yet a person will die much sooner from lack of water than from food shortage. In a temperate climate and consuming a diet providing about 2000 kcal, a person needs to consume over a litre of fluid per day in order to make good the losses which occur in the urine, faeces and by evaporation from the skin. The balance of water over and above that consumed as fluid comes from the water content of apparently solid food and the water produced as a result of the metabolism of carbohydrate, protein and fat.

Water loss is increased by a rise in the environmental temperature and in tropical countries can quickly produce a state of dehydration. The features appear sunken and the skin and tongue are dry. Dehydration sometimes occurs in elderly people because they do not drink sufficient fluid for fear of toilet difficulties. Some are incontinent and think that by reducing intake they will reduce embarrassment and difficulties caused by this problem. However, this is unlikely to be the case as there are many other causes of incontinence. They may, indeed, become confused as a result of dehydration.

Alcohol

Alcohol must be considered a food. The average consumption of alcohol in the United Kingdom amounts to approximately 20g per day for each adult. Based on an energy value of 7 kcal per g, this represents about 7 per cent of the mean dietary energy intake of the whole population. Many people will consume much more alcohol than this. A standard 0.7 litre bottle of spirits, containing 224g of alcohol, is theoretically equivalent to 1590 kcal. But it is now clear that we do not convert alcohol into as much energy as these figures suggest, at least in terms of its effect on body weight.

People who consume large amounts of alcohol sometimes become malnourished because alcoholic beverages are generally very poor sources of vitamins and minerals.

Chapter 3

Requirements and Allowances

We all need certain amounts of energy and nutrients to maintain health. To make sure that these requirements are met we need to eat foods which supply them. Foods differ in their content of different nutrients and a wide range of foods is needed to supply all the nutrients. Good nutrition is 'eating a little of everything and not too much of anything'.

The body's nutritional requirements will vary from one individual to another. For some nutrients, vitamin C for instance, the amount required to prevent a deficiency disease, in this case scurvy, has been determined by experiment. This 'requirement' has then been multiplied by three to take into account individual variations, reduced absorption and other factors which may increase the requirement, in order to arrive at a value which can be recommended as an 'allowance' to be provided for groups in the community. For other nutrients such as iron, the amount required to replace losses is used as a basis for calculating an 'allowance'. The proportion of dietary iron that is normally absorbed is about 10 per cent. Your diet should, therefore, contain ten times the amount required to replace losses. For other nutrients, the amount in the average diet of a large number of healthy people is used as a basis for a recommended allowance.

Tables of 'recommended daily amounts', 'recommended dietary allowances' (RDAs), or 'recommended dietary intakes' (RDIs) are produced by many governments. These tables are intended for use in relation to the diets of groups of people, not individuals, and are so calculated that they will prevent nutritional deficiency in at least 95 per cent of the population. With the exception of energy, the recommended amount of each nutrient includes a 'safety margin' so most people may consume amounts of nutrients that are below the RDAs. With the exception of energy, dietary intakes which are less than two-thirds of the RDA are likely to be deficient. Energy requirements vary much more widely than those of other nutrients. There is considerable variation in energy needs – people of the same body weight may require four times as much energy as others.

The amounts of dietary energy and protein recommended for males and females in the UK are shown in Table 3.1. The amounts increase with age and are higher in men than women because men have a larger lean body mass for their body weight than women. The recommended amounts are also increased for those in more active occupations and when there is a need to meet the extra demands of pregnancy and lactation.

Recommended daily amounts of vitamins and minerals are also shown in Table 3.1. Figures for some of these nutrients are not provided in the tables of recommended daily amounts published by the DHSS in the UK and have been taken from the corresponding publication of the US government. For some, but not all, of the nutrients the amounts are higher for males than for females and in females the amounts of most nutrients are increased during pregnancy and lactation.

For some nutrients, the amounts recommended in different countries vary considerably (see Table 3.2). These variations can be explained by the use of different criteria for defining adequacy. For example, in the UK, the RDA for vitamin C is based on the amount required to prevent scurvy, whereas in the US it is the amount required to maintain a saturation level in the tissues. Another factor that has been taken into account in proposing certain of these recommended amounts is the likelihood of being able to obtain the amount from what might be considered an average normal omnivorous diet. In other words, the RDAs must be realistic.

Table 3.1 Recommended daily amounts of energy and nutrients

Age (years) and occupational category	Energy* (kcal)	Protein* (g)	Vitamins		
			B_1* (mg)	B_2* (mg)	B_3* equivalents (mg)
Boys					
under 1	980	25	0.3	0.4	5
5–6	1740	43	0.7	0.9	10
12–14	2640	66	1.1	1.4	16
Girls					
under 1	910	25	0.3	0.4	5
5–6	1680	42	0.7	0.9	10
12–14	2150	53	0.9	1.4	16
Men					
18–34 Sedentary	2510	63	1.0	1.6	18
Moderately active	2900	72	1.2	1.6	18
Very active	3350	84	1.3	1.6	18
35–64 Sedentary	2400	60	1.0	1.6	18
Moderately active	2750	69	1.1	1.6	18
Very active	3350	84	1.3	1.6	18
65–74 Sedentary	2400	60	1.0	1.6	18
75+ Sedentary	2150	54	0.9	1.6	18
Women					
18–54 Most occupations	2150	54	0.9	1.3	15
Very active	2500	62	1.0	1.3	15
55–74 Sedentary	1900	47	0.8	1.3	15
75+ Sedentary	1680	42	0.7	1.3	15
Pregnancy	2400	60	1.0	1.6	18
Lactation	2750	69	1.1	1.8	21

* UK figures.

† USA figures.

table continues overleaf

B6† (mg)	B_{12}† (μg)	Folic acid† (μg)	C* (mg)	A* retinol equivalents (mg)	D* (μg)	E† (mg)
0.3	0.5–1.5	50	20	450	7.5	3–4
1.3	2.5	200	20	300	[a]	6
1.8	3.0	200	25	725	[a]	8
0.3	0.5–1.5	50	20	450	7.5	3–4
1.3	2.5	200	20	300	[a]	6
1.8	3.0	200	25	725	[a]	8
2.2	3.0	300	30	750	[a]	10
2.2	3.0	300	30	750	[a]	10
2.2	3.0	300	30	750	[a]	10
2.2	3.0	300	30	750	[a]	10
2.2	3.0	300	30	750	[a]	10
2.2	3.0	300	30	750	[a]	10
2.2	3.0	300	30	750	[a]	10
2.2	3.0	300	30	750	[a]	10
2.0	3.0	300	30	750	[a]	8
2.0	3.0	300	30	750	[a]	8
2.0	3.0	300	30	750	[a]	8
2.0	3.0	300	30	750	[a]	8
2.6	4.0	500	60	750	10	11
2.5	4.0	400	60	1200	10	11

[a] For children and adults who have sufficient exposure to sunlight no dietary sources of vitamin D may be necessary, but in winter children and adolescents should have 10mg daily by way of supplements. These supplements may also be required by adults who have inadequate exposure to sunlight, e.g. housebound.

Table 3.1 Recommended daily amounts of energy and nutrients (continued)

Age (years) and occupational category	Minerals		
	Calcium* (mg)	Iron* (mg)	Zinc† (mg)
Boys			
under 1	600	6	3–5
5–6	600	10	10
12–14	700	12	15
Girls			
under 1	600	6	3–5
5–6	600	10	10
12–14	700	12[c]	15
Men			
18–34 Sedentary	500	10	15
Moderately active	500	10	15
Very active	500	10	15
35–64 Sedentary	500	10	15
Moderately active	500	10	15
Very active	500	10	15
65–74 Sedentary	500	10	15
75+ Sedentary	500	10	15
Women			
18–54 Most occupations	500	12[c]	15
Very active	500	12[c]	15
55–74 Sedentary	500	10	15
75+ Sedentary	500	10	15
Pregnancy	1200[b]	13	20
Lactation	1200	15	25

[b] Extra calcium needed in the 3rd trimester, i.e. 6th to 9th month of pregnancy.

[c] This amount of iron may not be sufficient for 10% of girls and women who have large menstrual losses.

Table 3.2 Recommended intake of vitamins in the UK in comparison with those in other areas

Vitamin	Place			
	UK	EEC	USA	USSR
Vitamin B_1 (thiamine mg)	1.0	1.4	1.4	1.8
Vitamin B_2 (riboflavin mg)	1.6	1.6	1.6	2.4
Vitamin B_3 (nicotinic acid equiv. mg)	18	18	18	20
Vitamin C (ascorbic acid mg)	30	60	60	75
Vitamin A (retinol equiv. μg)	750	1000	1000	1500
Vitamin D (cholecalciferol μg)	–	5	5	12.5

It is also necessary to consider dietary pattern in relation to these allowances. It seems reasonable to suppose that nutrients will be utilized to maximum advantage if supplied at regular intervals through the day rather than in large amounts over a short period. Spacing your meals at intervals throughout the day is very important. Three meals per day is a reasonable pattern. However, some people find it suits their life-style best to have one large meal in the evening. But whatever you do, at each meal make absolutely sure you choose your foods from the food groups described in Chapters 1 and 7 (pp.3/85). If certain nutrients are not consumed at the same time your body will not be able to utilize them efficiently. For example, if the meal is based on pulses or nuts, the consumption of cereal foods will greatly enhance the quality of the protein in the meal. If the meal does not include any meat, vitamin C provided by fruit and vegetables will aid the absorption of iron from non-meat sources, bread, for example.

Chapter 4

Perspectives on Health Foods

The health-food industry is one of the fastest growing aspects of the present-day economy. Outlets are now found in most towns and their sales are still increasing. It is tempting to conclude that the consumption of the foods and supplements sold in health-food shops is simply a reflection of our interest in healthy living. However, things are not so simple.

We live in a technologically advanced country in which food is available in plenty, variety is immense and seasonally harvested food is marketed all the year round. This state of affairs is the result of the methods now available for the preservation and processing of food. The treatment of food in these ways naturally raises concerns in the minds of many people about possible effects on nutritional quality on the one hand, and the introduction of potentially undesirable compounds on the other. Most of us have a standard for food in our minds. There is no doubt that foods purchased fresh, or better still obtained fresh from the site of production, and cooked in the home under optimal conditions will be nutritionally, and probably aesthetically, better than food which has been stored for some time. It is, however, very easy to get the effects of preservation and processing out of proportion. We need to weigh these possible losses or dangers against their benefits.

But before considering the effects of these processes we should go further back in the food chain and mention other concerns which have played, and will continue to play, a part in stimulating the consumption of so-called 'health foods'. It is worth mentioning here that this term has no recognized precise definition other than that the foods are sold through health-food shops. Even this definition is now wanting in precision because the popularity of health foods has encouraged other kinds of shops, including pharmacies and supermarkets to sell them.

Food-chain influences

To return then, to the food chain. All our food, be it fruit, vegetables, dairy produce, eggs or meat, has its origin in plants. Farmers in western countries have been encouraged to try to increase their crops. In order to do this, increasing amounts of certain nutrients for plant crops in the form of chemical or artificial fertilizers have been used to stimulate plant growth and development. At the same time the growth of weeds that compete with food crops has been suppressed with herbicides and the growth of pests that damage or eat the crops has been suppressed with fungicides and insecticides. The use of all these chemical substances is carefully controlled by law. Nevertheless, their use has alarmed a number of people because of the possibility that small, but nevertheless potentially harmful amounts will persist as residues in the food when it is consumed. Worries such as these have stimulated interest in the growth of food without their use. Food grown in this way is often described as 'organically grown'. It is easy to see why such food might be sold in a health-food shop.

The principle of getting the most profit for the least outlay has not been restricted to plant crops. Chickens kept in a confined space with minimum scope for exercise but an abundance of food become egg-laying 'machines'. Though scientifically it has not proved possible to identify nutritionally important differences between eggs produced in this way and eggs laid by 'free-range' chickens, it must be admitted that the latter do at least have some aesthetic appeal. In addition, of course, is the question of taste, which is likely to be related to the feed provided for the chickens.

If we think of animals, such as pigs and cattle, reared for meat we are faced with another problem. It is well-known that certain hormones stimulate growth. If these are given to animals they improve the efficiency of conversion of feed into tissue, what is termed the 'food efficiency ratio'. This is clearly of benefit to the farmer in preparing animals for market. Further increases in the efficiency ratio may be obtained by suppressing the activity of pathogenic organisms, and drugs may be given for this purpose.

Now, the feared dangers of these procedures are that residues of the hormones or drugs may be found in the meat of the treated animals and that these, again, may cause ill-health in the consumer. Objections are again raised to the use of such methods on the ground that they are unnatural. Whatever the objection, there has been increasing interest in the natural rearing of domestic animals and meat from such animals is now being sold to those interested in, or concerned about, the effects of growth promoters on their health. Most people who eat 'natural-reared' meat would also say that the taste is better.

For some health-conscious people, however, the consumption of food of animal origin itself seems harmful to health and many persons who buy foods at health-food shops are vegetarians. Among the reasons that people give for becoming vegetarians, promotion of health, or 'because it makes me feel better', are commonly given. Many people who run health-food shops are themselves vegetarians.

Health foods

Whether we share these concerns and patronize health-food outlets or not, there is no doubt that many people claim that they 'feel better' as a result of consuming them. Such a response may be psychological rather than physiological. Many of the so-called 'health foods' carry misleading claims. Honey is a good example.

It has been claimed that honey has many nutritional virtues. However, analysis shows that it contains 20 per cent water and 75 per cent sugars with only small traces of minerals and vitamins. Cider vinegar and lecithin have been claimed to be 'aids' to weight reduction, but it is difficult to find evidence to support these claims.

However, to keep things in perspective, health-food outlets sell foods that are in line with dietary goals, for example, wholewheat bread, brown rice and wholewheat pasta. Another asset, is that they usually sell foods fortified with vitamin B_{12}, for example soyamilk, vegetable margarines and yeast extract. These foods are particularly important in the diet of strict vegetarians (vegans).

Vitamins

Many people take vitamin supplements which they purchase at inflated prices from health-food stores. Again, as with health foods, it may be difficult to argue against a subjective benefit. Claims are made that these supplements are needed to make good losses in foods due to preservatives or processing or to maintain what is described as 'optimum health' – not to be confused with the prevention of disease. The amounts of some vitamins that are consumed for these reasons often greatly exceed the recommended daily amounts (RDAs) and for this reason should more properly be considered pharmacological rather than nutritional. Some vitamins have toxic effects when consumed in large quantities (Table 4.1). There are some medical conditions which can be treated with large doses of vitamins. Chilblains is a condition which troubles many people and doses of nicotinic acid ('Pernivit') in excess of nutritional requirements may prove useful because it improves blood flow to the skin.

Table 4.1 Ill effects of high doses of some vitamins

B_3	Stomach ulcer; loss of hair; liver damage
B_6	Nerve damage and loss of balance
C	Kidney stones: scurvy-type symptoms when dose is reduced
A	Headaches: liver damage; skin changes: hair loss; tenderness of bones
D	Headaches; high blood pressure; deposits of calcium in soft tissues such as the kidneys
E	Tendency to bleeding when taken with the drug warfarin (used in the treatment of coronary heart disease)
K	A type of anaemia in which blood cells are destroyed

Effects of preservation, processing and cooking

There are beneficial effects of food processing. For many of us, legumes, particularly peas and different varieties of beans are important constituents in our diet. Most legumes contain a number of toxins and substances which inhibit the activity of digestive enzymes and particularly trypsin. The toxins in soya beans are easily destroyed by heat, whereas those in other beans, such as lima beans and green gram, are very heat stable. If the beans are heated for longer than to destroy the toxins, the quality of the protein is reduced.

Other toxins in legumes include substances which affect the thyroid gland (goitrogens) and others which cause red cells to agglutinate (such as lectins). These substances which are harmful to human health are destroyed by appropriate processing thus making the vegetables safe for consumption.

Vitamin B_3 is present in many cereals in a bound form which is not absorbed unless previously liberated by heat, such as during baking and under alkaline conditions.

A detailed discussion of the effects of the various methods of processing food – pasteurization, drying, canning, freezing, irradiation – or of cooking – boiling, pressure cooking and microwave heating – on nutritional quality are outside the scope of this book. The effects of these processes on individual vitamins – the nutrients likely to be most affected – are shown in Table 4.2

Table 4.2 Stability of vitamins

C (Ascorbic acid) Most vulnerable to cooking conditions. Readily destroyed by exposure to air and readily soluble in water. Losses minimized by preparing vegetables immediately before cooking, boiling in the minimum quantity of water, for the shortest time, and serving when ready.

B_1 (Thiamine) Sensitive to heat and alkaline or neutral conditions. Losses of 10–20% may be expected on cooking. Losses increased by baking powder and by sulphite used as a preservative in some foods.

B_2 (Riboflavin) Sensitive to light. 50% of B_2 in milk may be lost if kept in the sun for 2 hours. About 20% may be lost on a dull day.

B_6 (Pyridoxine) Sensitive to heat. Substantial amount destroyed by canning and sterilization and in the drying of milk.

B_{12} (Cyanocobalamin) Stable when meat or liver are cooked under ordinary conditions. Water soluble and therefore may be lost in drippings. In milk, pasteurization destroys 7%, boiling for 3 minutes destroys 30% and ultra-heat treatment destroys 20% of the vitamin activity.

Folate Rapidly destroyed by heat in alkaline or neutral conditions. About 50% lost in canning and after cooking of vegetables. Losses in cooking meat and eggs usually less.

Vitamin A and carotene Stable during mild heat treatment. Losses occur at high temperatures. Protected by antioxidants in foods including vitamin E.

Vitamin E Slowly destroyed by heat during frying. Sensitive to light. Unstable in fried foods during frozen storage.

Concern is expressed about the effects of irradiation as a means of preserving food. Different doses have been recommended for different foods and for different purposes, including inhibition of sprouting, delaying the ripening of fruits and elimination of parasites and pathogens. The recommended dose is, according to our present knowledge, safe and nutrient losses are similar to those caused by other kinds of processing in widespread use.

Food additives

Concern of a different sort is sometimes felt about a range of compounds collectively known as 'food additives'. These compounds are added to foods by manufacturers for a number of purposes. Some are colorants, whilst others are preservatives, antioxidants and flavourings. Not all substances added to food are artificial in the sense that they have been synthesized by a chemist or natural products that have been modified in some way by a chemist. Some are naturally occurring compounds that are added to foods to flavour them or to increase their nutritional value. This distinction between 'artificial' and 'natural' has been played up by 'natural food' enthusiasts but is often quite nonsensical. For example, L-ascorbic acid (vitamin C) is chemically the same compound whether it is synthesized in a factory or extracted from a natural source. It has the same properties whatever its origin. People should not be persuaded to pay a higher price for the 'natural' substance.

There is no doubt that popular interest in food additives has been increased by the use of 'E numbers' to describe them. This system is used by the EEC to identify permitted additives distinctly within the multilingual Common Market. Maurice Hansson's book *E for Additives* is a layman's guide to the chemical identity of each E number. Some examples are given in Table 4.3. Many people will avoid any product which contains any E numbers on the label regardless of their chemical identity.

Table 4.3 The identity of some common E numbers

E number	Substance
Antioxidants	
E300	L-Ascorbic acid
E301	Sodium L-ascorbate
E306	Extracts of natural origin rich in tocopherols
E307	Synthetic α-tocopherol
E310	Propyl gallate
E320	Butylated hydroxyanisole (BHA)
E321	Butylated hydroxytoluene (BHT)
E322	Lecithins
Colours	
E100	Curcumin
E101	Riboflavin
E102	Tartrazine
E110	Sunset yellow FCF
E120	Cochineal
E122	Carmoisine
E124	Ponceau 4R
E127	Erythrosine
E142	Green S
E150	Caramel
E153	Carbon black (vegetable carbon)
E154	Brown FK
E155	Brown HT (chocolate brown HT)
E162	Beetroot red (betanin)
E163	Anthocyanins
Emulsifiers and stabilizers	
E400	Alginic acid
E406	Agar
E407	Carrageenan
E410	Locust bean gum (carob gum)
E412	Guar gum
E413	Tragacanth
E414	Gum arabic (acacia)
E440(a)	Pectin
E440(b)	Amidated pectin, pectin extract
E461	Methylcellulose
E470	Sodium, potassium and calcium salts of fatty acids
E474	Sucroglycerides
E477	Propane-1, 2-diol esters of fatty acids
Preservatives	
E200	Sorbic acid
E210	Benzoic acid
E211	Sodium benzoate
E219	Methyl 4-hydroxy benzoate, sodium salt
E220	Sulphur dioxide
E221	Sodium sulphite
E227	Calcium hydrogen sulphite
E252	Potassium nitrate
E280	Propionic acid
E283	Potassium propionate
Sweeteners	
E421	Mannitol
E420	Sorbitol

Colours, and more recently, particularly the orange dye, tartrazine (E102), were suggested by the late Dr Ben Feingold to be a cause of hyperactivity in children. Whilst lack of satisfactory proof of such a link led the Nutrition Foundation in the US to infer that they did not cause problems, there is no doubt that they may cause problems in a few children. If you happen to be the parent of one of these susceptible children the harmful effect of the colorant is extremely important. We would seriously advise any parent of a hyperactive child who consumes highly coloured drinks or lollies or similar products, to test the child for themselves by omitting the products and noting any difference in the child's behaviour. However, such testing must be done with great care. It is, alas, all too easy for parents to attribute their child's naughtiness to the 'nasty things' that food manufacturers put in our foods. Or, indeed, to conclude that a child is allergic to a particular food or foods with a resulting restriction of the child's diet. What have been called 'pseudo food allergies' are potentially a real nutritional problem. Moreover, they may cause considerable psychological damage because the child is made to feel 'different' and deprived.

Chapter 5

What Do Food Labels Tell You?

To choose food wisely it is useful to read food labels. The information presented is meant to help you make an informed choice between all the various foods available. Certain details are required by law:

1 *Name of food* – Prepacked foods and the majority of non-prepacked foods must show the name of the food. The name should not in any way mislead the consumer. For example a raspberry yogurt can only be called 'raspberry', 'raspberry flavoured' or have a picture of raspberries on the label if flavoured with real raspberries. If the flavour does not mainly come from raspberries the product should be called 'raspberry flavour' yogurt. The name given to the food should also state the condition of the product, for example 'powdered'.

2 *Net quantity* – Prepacked food with some exceptions such as eggs and flour confectionery, must show the net quantity by weight or volume.

3 *List of ingredients* – Most prepacked foods must include a list of ingredients which should appear in descending order of weight. If more than 5% of the food product consists of added water this must be included. If a particular ingredient is emphasized, for example apple tart with extra fruit, then the percentage must be shown on the label.

4 *Minimum durability* – Most foods are date marked, but foods which will keep longer than eighteen months do not have to carry a

date mark. Date marks are usually 'Best before' followed by day, month and year. The year may be omitted if the food will not keep for more than three months. If the food will keep for more than three months the day may be omitted. If this is the case 'Best before end' is used, followed by month and year. If the food is perishable it may be marked 'Sell by' followed by the latest recommended date of sale. Food labels should also indicate the number of days within which the food is best eaten, giving any required storage conditions.

5 *Special conditions of storage* – Date marks are based on the assumptions that foods will be stored properly for example 'in a cool, dry place'.

6 *Name and address of manufacturer or packer or distributor* – The people responsible for the original condition of the food may need to be contacted if the food is not up to standard.

7 *Place of origin* – If people are likely to be misled about the origin of a food the place where the food comes from should be stated on the label.

8 *Instructions for use* – These should be included if the food is difficult to use without them.

What about the nutritional quality of food?

Our tables giving the nutritional value of food portions in Chapter 8 are comprehensive, dealing with some 600 foods. But, since new foods are being developed all the time you need to know how to assess the nutritional quality of food by interpreting food labels. These vary in the amount and type of nutrition information given. This aspect of food labelling is currently being looked into by various committees. To get the general picture about nutritional quality three particular parts of food labels are worth looking at (see Fig. 5.1).

Ingredients Ingredient lists tell you what has been used in the food product. As previously mentioned the ingredients are listed in

Figure 5.1 What to look for to assess nutritional quality

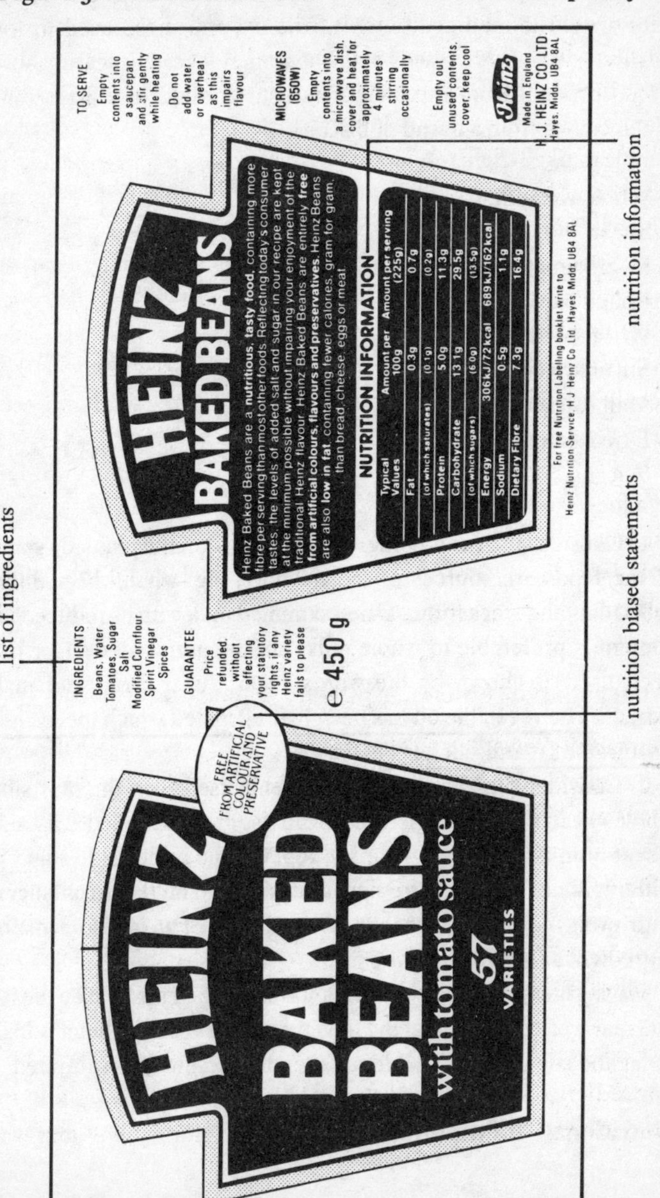

order of weight merit. The ingredients used in the highest quantities are positioned at the top of the list and those used in the smallest amounts are placed at the bottom. A lot can be learnt about a food product from the ingredient list. Consider the list below, which comes from a brand of biscuit.

Wholewheat flour
Sugar
Hydrogenated vegetable oil
Rolled oats
Wheat bran
Sugar syrup
Malt extract
Dried skimmed milk
Salt

1 Consider the types of ingredients used – on the plus side some of the foods are sources of dietary fibre, e.g. wholewheat flour, rolled oats and wheat bran. Dried skimmed milk with its reduced fat content is preferable to whole milk. On the minus side sugar has been used as shown by the words sugar, sugar syrup and malt extract. The vegetable oil has been hydrogenated which means it is a saturated fat and salt has been used.

2 Consider the quantity of ingredients used – on the plus side wholewheat flour is at the top of the list and the rolled oats and wheat bran are relatively near the top. On the minus side sugar is without doubt a major ingredient as it is second on the list as 'sugar' with even more sugar further down the list. Fat is also a major ingredient as it is third on the list.

Having identified the ingredients and noted their position on the list you may well conclude that the food provides some fibre but it is high in fat and sugar, contains added salt and the fat used is saturated.

Nutritional information Nutritional information may be

presented in various ways. Nutrients are usually expressed in any one or more of the following combinations:

per serving
per 100g
percentage RDAs per serving

Nutrients per serving are relatively easy to understand. You can compare the figures with your own RDA or extract the information you require to complete your nutrition profile.

Nutrients per 100g are not so easy to deal with because you will need to find out the weight of your food portion. When you know the weight you can use the figures presented to calculate what is in your portion of food.

The percentage of the RDA provided by a portion of food is useful because you can tell straightaway if nutrients are present in significant amounts.

Statements with a nutritional bias Some food labels boast all manner of 'nutritional attributes'. These need to be interpreted with a certain amount of caution.

Consider the following examples:

'Haricot beans are a valuable natural food, rich in protein and nutrients and high in fibre. Ready prepared using honey and natural sea salt . . .'

The product is a useful source of protein and fibre and nutrients in general, but which ones? Added sugar and salt have been used; do not be misled by the words 'honey' and 'natural sea salt'.

'Carrots are a valuable source of vitamin A which we need regularly to keep the skin healthy and generally improve our resistance to infection. One serving of carrots provides all the daily requirements of this essential vitamin.'

The product is clearly a useful source of vitamin A. You are also reminded of the functions of this nutrient.

Chapter 6

Food Choice: Variations in Diet

There may be very specific reasons why people's eating habits differ from the 'norm'. It is useful to know something about this if you are involved in planning meals for such people, or you may wish or need to change your own diet. It is convenient to consider this topic under four main headings:

1 Population groups with special needs
2 Unusual diets
3 Diet in the treatment of some common diseases
4 Diet during convalescence from illness

Population groups with special needs

Some people are described as being nutritionally vulnerable because they may be at risk for developing nutritional deficiencies.

Babies It is currently recommended by the Department of Health and Social Security (DHSS), that 'Mothers should be encouraged to continue breastfeeding for longer than three months as long as the baby continues to thrive.' Breastfeeding has very definite advantages for both mother and baby of which parents should be aware. But for those mothers who do not wish to breastfeed or for some reason cannot do so there are alternatives based on humanized cow's milk, which, if used correctly carry little health risk. The DHSS recommends that solid food should be introduced between 3 and 6 months according to baby's progress. Solids, such as cereals, should not be given before the age of three months because of the underdevelopment of the baby's immune system and the possibility of causing allergies. Milk is not a good source of iron. The iron store in a newborn baby is only sufficient for about three to four months. So it is important to introduce foods rich in iron during weaning. It is known that a baby's taste preferences are established in infancy. For this reason it is recommended that added salt and salty foods should be avoided, as too should sugar and sugary foods.

Young children Whilst children should gradually become accustomed to a diet containing roughage, over-zealous parents may push these recommendations too far with the result that they develop what has been aptly described as the 'muesli belt syndrome' with an extended abdomen and associated malnutrition. The safest plan is gradually to change the diet as the child gets older. In our view no attempt should be made to feed young pre-school children on a high-fibre low-fat diet. If low-fat milks are given, for example, skimmed or semi-skimmed, the fat-soluble vitamins A and D are lost. All infants and young children should receive adequate vitamins. A vitamin supplement is particularly important for low-birth-weight babies, Asian children and all those who have limited sources of vitamin D. Excess vitamin D is toxic and has been known to cause severe illness and even death. Supplements should generally be taken only under medical or nursing supervision.

Adolescents The feeding habits of adolescents are commonly characterized by bizarre eating periods, slimming fads, irregular meals and living on snacks and convenience foods. It has been estimated that 1 in 100 girls has severe anorexia nervosa and that many other girls have at some time tried severe slimming programmes, lost weight or induced voluntary vomiting. Although much less common, these problems can also occur in boys. Anorectics develop a phobia about carbohydrate-rich foods because they are associated in their minds with body fat. The development of this phobia is a danger signal and so too, in girls, is the cessation of the menstrual cycle.

Eating for health involves sufficient food of the right kind to provide all the energy and nutrients required to maintain normal body weight. Phobias about certain foods are likely to cause nutrient deficiencies. Weight-conscious adolescents should welcome the recommendation to reduce the amount of fat in the diet. However unacceptable it may seem, they must appreciate that the recommendation to eat more fibre-rich complex carbohydrate applies as much to them as to the rest of society.

Adolescents are particularly 'at risk' nutritionally if they become pregnant. The problems associated with their dietary habits are further exacerbated by the fact that they, as well as the baby, are growing, and also often by their inadequate social and economic circumstances.

Women of child-bearing age About 1 in 10 women of child-bearing age are anaemic due to a dietary deficiency of iron. Either the amount of iron in the diet is insufficient to meet the demands of menstruation, or iron is present in the diet in a form which is not well absorbed. In addition, many women become anaemic during pregnancy, again due to the supply of iron not being sufficient to meet the requirements. Iron supplements are often prescribed to treat the anaemia. However, careful choice of iron-rich foods could, in most women, prevent the condition. Moreover, it would do so without running the risk of interactions between minerals in the gut which can result when iron supplements are taken. If the extra need for iron is met by including liver in the diet, the iron is readily absorbed. Liver is also a good source of folic acid which is needed in greater than normal amounts during pregnancy.

It is possible that vitamin deficiencies in the mother at the time of conception may increase the risk of developing defects such as spina bifida and anencephaly in the fetus. Evidence at present suggests that deficiency of one or more vitamins of the B group may be involved. It would seem prudent to ensure that an intending mother has a good diet before, as well as after, she conceives.

The elderly The elderly are defined by the ages at which a state pension can be drawn. It is quite evident that they are far from being a homogeneous group and age alone may give no clue to their health. Dietary goals cannot be applied to older people indiscriminately. Whilst it is likely that bowel action will be improved in all of them by persuading them to take a high-fibre breakfast cereal and to eat wholemeal bread, dietary habits of a lifetime may be difficult to change. Moreover, such changes are likely to have undesirable consequences amongst those older people who are recognized as being at risk of malnutrition – the physically and mentally disabled, the housebound and socially isolated, widowers and the very old. Poor food intake is unlikely to be helped by a high-roughage diet and an already low energy intake by a reduction in fat. Moreover, reducing the fat intake may well mean that they become even more at risk of vitamin D deficiency.

Unusual diets

There is no single 'ideal' or 'healthy' diet. A wide variety of dietary practices are followed in the UK. Some of the extreme ones have associated health problems. As a general principle and guideline it should be remembered that if the variety of foods consumed is reduced we need to know more about the composition of foods in order that those consumed should supply adequate amounts of energy and all the nutrients.

For the purposes of this chapter we will consider that the omnivorous diet is the usual one. A meat-containing diet is certainly the most widely catered for in the UK but it is by no means acceptable to all the population. It is, therefore, necessary to consider alternative diets, most of which involve some form of vegetarianism. In a country with a number of different ethnic groups it is not surprising that there are diets that are peculiar to these groups as they seek to maintain their national, cultural and religious characteristics. All those interested in 'healthy eating' should understand the advantages and limitations of some of these dietary variations.

If people do adopt restricted diets, nutritional inadequacies may well take a long time to manifest themselves in adults. But babies, young children and pregnant and lactating women are particularly vulnerable to dietary deficiencies. Exaggerating any aspect of a diet can cause problems. We have already mentioned the problem caused in young children by over-zealous emphasis on dietary fibre. This has an effect on nutrient density with the possibility of preventing absorption of some minerals and causing malnutrition.

We will now briefly discuss the nutritional aspects of vegetarianism, the diets favoured by ethnic minorities and two restrictive dietary practices, Zen macrobiotic and fruitarian, that are followed by some people in the UK.

Vegetarianism People who claim to be 'vegetarians' vary considerably in the foods that they will eat. Strict vegetarians, or vegans, do not consume any foods of animal origin. In addition to the total exclusion of meat, eggs and milk and all dairy products are avoided. These last-named foods are consumed by lacto-ovo-vegetarians, and pescovegetarians consume fish.

Vegetarians Not unexpectedly, the nutritional quality of a vegetarian diet may vary much more than that of an omnivorous diet. If dairy produce is included then the nutrient content may be similar to that of the average non-vegetarian diet. People who do not eat dairy produce and eggs are at risk of not having sufficient vitamin B_{12} and calcium, and in children the vitamin D intake may give cause for concern.

A large number of people in the UK are vegetarians and these include a number of ethnic groups. Among the latter are those who eat a vegetarian diet for cultural or religious reasons and these will be considered later.

Amongst the indigenous population there is no doubt that a vegetarian diet is increasing in popularity and particularly so amongst professional people and the more highly educated. Practitioners of homeopathy, osteopathy and naturopathy often recommend a vegetarian diet. To some vegetarians, it is not just the diet which is important but their whole way of life, and they may be more health-conscious, taking frequent exercise, and abstaining from alcohol and smoking. Indeed, health may be one important reason why vegetarians have chosen the diet. Philosophical and ethical considerations may also be important. Some vegetarians seem to be somewhat evangelistic in popularizing the health-giving properties of their diet and there is some evidence that they suffer less frequently from intestinal diseases. It is tempting to attribute this finding to their high intake of dietary fibre. If a high intake of roughage should be desirable, and it is one of the NACNE recommendations, there is, in fact no need to adopt a vegetarian, much less a vegan diet in order to obtain it. A high intake of unrefined cereals with plenty of vegetables will lead to an increase in dietary fibre. It may be a surprise to learn that some omnivores consume rather more roughage than vegetarians by an addiction to particular breakfast cereals. The fat content of vegetarian diets is very variable and ethnic and cultural variations in the food eaten may mean that at least as great a percentage of energy in the vegetarian, as in the omnivorous diet, comes from fat.

Vegans Vegans tend to be slimmer than vegetarians and their diets almost always contain less energy, protein, fat, calcium, vitamins D, B_{12} and riboflavin but more unsaturated fatty acids, vitamin C, vitamin A and folate, and more iron, fibre and unrefined carbohydrate. They also contain very little cholesterol. Because of its low total fat, low cholesterol and high polyunsaturated fatty acid and fibre content, a vegan diet could be useful in lowering plasma cholesterol levels.

Of course, all the protein in a vegan diet comes from plant foods, but provided that it comes from a mixture of cereals, nuts and pulses, the amino acid profile of the diet will be satisfactory. Proteins from these three plant groups complement each other. Soya protein, in particular, is a good source of 'essential' amino acids.

Although the iron content of vegan diets tends to be higher than that of non-vegetarians the iron is not present in the most readily absorbed form. This, together with the usually higher phytate content of the diet might make one think that vegans would tend to be anaemic. There seems to be no evidence that this is so. The high vitamin C content of the diet may offset the effect of the phytate by facilitating the absorption of iron.

Vegans are advised to take supplements or to eat foods fortified with vitamin B_{12}, see Chapter 4 (p.37). There is no reason why female vegans should not produce normal healthy offspring, but vitamin B_{12} and riboflavin supplementation are strongly recommended during lactation. If mothers cannot breastfeed their babies soya-based modified milk formulas are available. These include Velactin (Wander), Prosobee (Mead Johnson), Wysoy (Wyeth) and Formula S (Cow & Gate).

The diets of ethnic minorities It is understandable that those who have come to live here from parts of the old British Empire should wish to follow the dietary practices that developed from their ethnic culture, religion and customs. Indeed to do so contributes greatly to their quality of life and the development of community. Within a given minority, however, there are considerable variations in food choice and these can to some extent be explained by the 'three generation concept'.

The first generation is deemed to consist of migrants who came as dependent relatives of migrant workers. These are now mostly retired people who prefer to eat their native dishes rather than adapt to British-style foods. Others of this generation are migrant workers themselves. They are classified as being in an age range of twenty-one to sixty-five years and generally accept British food and their ethnic foods equally.

The second generation are the young people aged seven to twenty-one years who went to school here. They were also born here and prefer a British diet. This generation tends to resist attempts to get them to follow an ethnic diet.

The third generation are children, who feel British but become interested in tracing their roots. They are therefore interested in eating ethnic as well as British food.

It is interesting that cultural differences in food are accompanied by differences in feeding habits. Thus, whereas Europeans use a fork to eat rice, Afro-Caribbeans and Asians use a spoon and the Chinese prefer chopsticks. First and third generation ethnic minority groups may follow ethnic custom whereas the second generation will tend to follow their European peers. Some ethnic Asians and Afro-Caribbeans may prefer to use their hands for some foods. According to religious and cultural customs they wash their hands before eating, and after eating they not only wash their hands again but also rinse their mouths, thus cleaning their teeth.

Some ethnic groups have definite views about the relationship of food to health. Asian healers such as Hakims and Vaids were aware of food allergies and used to practise the omission of certain foods in treating any disease. Sick Asians seeing a doctor may well ask what foods they should avoid.

In Afro-Asian cultures, milk, orange juice, lemonade and Ribena are considered to aggravate colds and coughs, whereas hot curries and meat dishes are considered 'hot' and therefore beneficial in treating these conditions.

It should be remembered that most non-Caucasian adults are lactose intolerant. Milk will sometimes cause diarrhoea and vomiting.

Cassava is mainly eaten by Africans whereas chapati is eaten exclusively by ethnic Asians and is their main bread. Chapati flour contains phytic acid which forms an insoluble complex, calcium phytate, with calcium. This factor, together with a low vitamin D content of the diet and limited exposure to sunlight probably accounts for the presence of rickets in Asian children and osteomalacia in adults.

Ethnic Asian groups Amongst Asian people there are a number of religions that influence the foods that their followers eat.

To *Muslims*, eating is seen as a worship of Allah. According to the Quran, there are two types of food. *Haram* is prohibited and *halal* is lawful. Muslims are not allowed to eat pork or drink alcohol. Meat and animal fats have to be prepared ritually, according to the Islamic faith, in order to be *halal*. In order to be acceptable to Muslims convenience baby foods must be made from *halal* constituents.

Hindus follow *ahisma* – they do not kill animals for food. Certain foods, including beef, pork, lamb, chicken and fish are strictly forbidden. Dairy produce and eggs are consumed by most, but not all, Hindus. Those of higher castes are often strict vegetarians.

Sikhism combines certain concepts of Hinduism and Islam. Sikhs do not eat beef and rarely eat pork. Many Sikhs are lacto-vegetarians.

Buddhists eat a rice-based diet with meat and fish eaten exceptionally and only when the animals have not been killed specifically for eating.

Early introduction of cow's milk with its lower iron content compared with breast or formula milk increases the risk of anaemia in Asian infants. Those parents who are strict vegetarians will have some difficulty in their choice of prepared baby foods because a number of these contain meat or meat extracts. There is always a risk of causing a degree of malnutrition in their children if infants are weaned on to starchy high roughage foods.

Reference has already been made to the risk of vitamin D deficiency in Asian children. Iron deficiency can also occur in vegetarian Hindus as well as a type of anaemia due to lack of dietary vitamin B_{12}.

Immigrants from India have a high death rate from coronary heart disease but this seems not to be related to their fat intake. Interestingly, the fat intake of vegetarian and non-vegetarian households was found to be similar amongst the Gujaratis, Punjabis, Southern Indians and Muslims investigated. It is also of interest that vegetarianism, as practised in Asian groups, in contrast to that practised amongst the indigenous population, does not appear to protect them against obesity.

Afro-Caribbean The traditional Afro-Caribbean diet consists mainly of pork, chicken, rice and peas and bananas. The attraction of this diet is that it is economical and easy to prepare and it has a high-fibre content. However, large amounts of salt are consumed along with herbs and spices. Afro-Caribbeans are predisposed to the development of high blood pressure which may well be due to a genetic hypersensitivity to salt.

Rastafarianism, a religious sect started in Jamaica, has now spread to Europe and appears to be increasingly popular amongst young black people in the UK. Rastafarian dietary practices vary considerably. The male is dominant in the family and follows the diet rigidly, insisting that his children do the same. To be acceptable to Rasta, foods must be 'total' or 'natural'. Rastafarians refer to such foods as I-tal. Foods of animal origin are regarded as 'dead' and undesirable; foods of vegetable origin are 'I-tal'. The Old Testament is also used as a source of food laws. Meat is considered of no benefit and orthodox Rastafarians are, in fact, vegans, but often do not have the knowledge of foods necessary to follow such a diet satisfactorily. They tend to have an aversion to taking vitamin B_{12} supplements and because their cooking procedures involve prolonged cooking with the discarding of cooking water, folic acid deficiency may well contribute to the development of megaloblastic anaemia.

Children weaned on to a strict Rastafarian diet consisting only of I-tal foods are at risk of developing rickets and iron deficiency. The health of Rastafarian mothers may well be at risk because the diet is nutritionally too poor to meet the demands of pregnancy and subsequent prolonged breastfeeding.

Restrictive dietary practices Fads and fallacies abound in nutrition and the number of 'quack' diets is legion. 'Slimming' is a popular money-making racket with people being encouraged to follow all sorts of restrictive diets. To do so without sound medical or dietetic advice often carries health risks. Ideas that certain foods are 'fattening' or that they have adverse effects, what have been termed 'pseudo-allergies', can lead to serious nutritional deficiencies. We all know teenage girls who, having become obsessed with their weight, have gone too far, developed a phobia about the 'fattening' qualities of carbohydrate and have developed the disease, anorexia nervosa. This has become frighteningly common. Once developed with all its psychiatric problems, it is very difficult to treat and individuals usually need special help and advice which involves the whole family.

Food choices may also be restricted due to cultural influences or for philosophical reasons, e.g. the Zen macrobiotic diet. Often these restrictions are made in the belief that there is some advantage for health. Individual foods are held to be responsible for a whole variety of human ills, but some of the resulting diets are nutritionally unsound and dangerous, particularly for children. Indeed, parents who feed their children such diets may well be guilty, in the eyes of the law, of cruelty. Two diets are worthy of comment here, just to illustrate the point we are making.

Zen macrobiotic diet The Zen macrobiotic diet was popularized by George Oshawa (1893–1966) and can be restrictive. It is based on whole-grain cereals supplemented with beans and vegetables. Processed foods, alcoholic and caffeine-containing drinks are all avoided. Indeed, drinking liquids of any description is restricted. There are ten diets that are rated from −3 to 7 and become increasingly restricted with diet 7 composed only of whole grain cereals. Followers of the macrobiotic way of life and of these regimes use tables which show the percentage of foods in various food groups which make up different diets. Whole-grain rice is the preferred cereal. Normally two-thirds of the daily vegetables are cooked and one-third eaten raw. Animal foods are only permitted in diets −3 to 2. Nutritional problems increase as one proceeds up the grades. Strict adherence to diet 7 can result in scurvy, anaemia, hypoproteinaemia, hypocalcaemia and loss of kidney function. Children given these diets can become very ill with kwashiorkor, anaemia and risk of cardiac failure. Parents who follow the Zen macrobiotic philosophy should be encouraged to give their children diets within the lower numbers.

Fruitarian diet The fruitarian diet is a highly restricted vegan diet with only fruit, nuts and seeds being eaten, normally uncooked. Extremely careful planning is essential if this diet is to be in any way nutritionally adequate. Vitamin supplements (B_{12}, riboflavin and vitamin D) are advisable, and in order to meet requirements for vitamin A, fruit sources of the pro-vitamin β-carotene should be eaten. These fruits – melons, apricots and mangoes – can be expensive in the UK.

Diet in the treatment of some common diseases

In our discussion of nutrients reference was made to diseases caused by a deficiency of particular nutrients. Dietary modifications are essential in the control or management of certain other diseases either because the body is not able to metabolize certain constituents of foods or because the body's functioning has been so deranged by disease (e.g. failure of a particular organ such as the kidneys) that it cannot deal with a normal intake of one or more nutrients. These aspects of nutrition are rightly the responsibility of a therapeutic dietitian who may specialize in a group of diseases, like those described as 'inborn errors of metabolism', or a particular organ, like the kidney. The principal features of the dietary management of some common diseases are given in Table 6.1. It is not intended that this should in any way be a 'do it yourself' manual. Persons with one of these diseases should be under the care of a qualified dietitian. What we are giving here are a few principles which may help you to understand the basis for the dietetic advice that you have received.

Table 6.1 Summary of diseases treated by dietary modifications

Phenylketonuria Absence of enzyme required for the metabolism and utilization of the amino acid, phenylalanine. Amino acid accumulates in the blood stream and causes brain damage. Now diagnosed soon after birth.
Dietary modification Low phenylalanine intake. 'Essential' amino acid, therefore must provide some for growth.
Galactosaemia Absence of enzyme required for the metabolism and utilization of a sugar, galactose, which is a constituent of milk sugar, lactose. Galactose accumulates in the blood stream and causes brain damage. Diagnosed in early life.
Dietary modification Milk-free diet.
Lactose intolerance Absence or low activity of the enzyme which splits lactose in to its constituent sugars, glucose and galactose, in the intestine. Dietary lactose causes diarrhoea. Characteristic of adult non-Caucasians.
Dietary modification Limited milk consumption.
Cardiovascular disease Many factors are probably involved in

causing cardiovascular disease. 'Healthy eating' aimed at primary prevention. In persons who have already had a 'coronary' blood lipids may be high. Blood may have tendency to clot too rapidly. Aim of changes is secondary prevention, i.e. prevent further problems. Obesity and hypertension contributing factors.

Dietary modification Reduce body weight if above 'normal' for height. Reduce total fat intake by reducing saturated (animal) fat. Increase dietary fibre, particularly fruit and wheat. Increase consumption of fatty fish (herring and mackerel).

Take moderate, regular exercise. Stop smoking.

Diabetes mellitus Due to a variety of underlying causes. Characterized by raised glucose concentration in the blood due to a deficiency or diminished effectiveness of insulin, a hormone produced in the pancreas.

Dietary modification Treated with diet alone, diet and drugs or diet and insulin. Amount and nature of carbohydrate controlled. Intake of refined sugars reduced and of unrefined increased. Aim is to control the blood glucose level and reduce incidence of complications. Patients who are overweight should reduce.

Gout An arthritis which affects single joints. Associated with the deposition of urate crystals and raised blood uric acid concentration.

Dietary modification Overweight patients should reduce their weight. Excessive alcohol drinking should be avoided. A low purine diet – less meat, especially offal, may help.

Chronic renal failure (uraemia) Chronic failure of the kidneys is the final common result of a number of diseases. The ability of the kidneys to remove end-products of protein metabolism from the blood is reduced. Consequently these accumulate in the blood.

Dietary modification A number of different forms of treatment – kidney transplants, dialysis and diet – are available. Diet is low in protein – restricted to provision of essential amino acids, and high in energy. Aim is to provide amino acids for tissue maintenance and repair only and all energy from other sources.

Hiatus hernia Upper part of the stomach pushed up through the diaphragm and therefore caused by increased abdominal pressure. May be the result of obesity or straining to empty the bowels.

Dietary modification If obese, weight should be reduced with low energy diet. Increase dietary fibre to facilitate passage of stools.

Gallbladder disease, gallstones Inflammation of the gall-bladder usually associated with the presence of stones in the gallbladder.

Dietary modification Foods which aggravate symptoms should be avoided. These include cooked meats rich in fat and fried foods. Moderate intake of uncooked fat, e.g. milk, butter and cream cheese, permitted. Avoid large meals.

Coeliac disease (gluten-sensitive enteropathy) Sensitivity to gluten, a main constituent of wheat flour results in flattening of intestinal villi with consequent malabsorption.

Dietary modification Gluten-free diet restores normal villi.

Cancer Many patients are malnourished. Disturbances in carbohydrate and protein metabolism occur. Low food intake due to anorexia and changes in taste. Effects of tumour exacerbated by treatment.

Dietary modification Food may need to be nutrient-dense to cater for small appetite. Food to be taken little and often. Normal food may need to be supplemented by sip feeds or tube feeding.

Surgery and injury Trauma from whatever cause results in metabolic changes that ensure increased energy production and limit fluid losses. Magnitude of changes proportional to severity of injury. Patients cannibalize own tissues. If not fed they become malnourished. Tissue breakdown increased by sepsis. Losses greatest in burned patients.

Dietary modification Provision of adequate nutrition important for convalescence. Supplemental feeding through nasogastric tube or total feeding by vein may be necessary.

Food 'allergies' Adverse reactions to food have been claimed to

cause diseases in all body systems. Psychological factors, genetic defects, hypersensitivity to chemicals in foods and reactions involving the immune system.
Dietary modification Identification of foods by direct challenge with subsequent omission of foods causing reactive effects may result in total cure.

The treatment of many diseases involves the regular taking of a variety of drugs. Patients are instructed to take some drugs before, with or after meals. This is because food may have a variable effect on the absorption, and hence the effect of drugs. Observing these instructions is thus important if the desired therapeutic effect of the drug is to be obtained. In addition, some drugs may increase the requirement for certain nutrients because they decrease their absorption, interfere with their metabolism or increase their excretion.

Diet during convalescence from illness

If you are convalescing after a serious illness you may be advised to have a 'light' diet. There is no reason why this should not be a healthy one. Indeed, it is essential that you consume enough energy and all the other nutrients to restore damaged tissues and normal body function. This may well take a considerable time depending on the severity of the illness. It is important that food intake is increased gradually. The maxim 'little and often' may need to be followed in order to achieve an acceptable intake. You should avoid sloppy or soft foods. Examples of suitable meals are: Breakfast – orange juice, porridge made with milk; Lunch – grilled chicken with mashed potatoes and green salad; Supper – milky drink, wholewheat bread with fruit spread, wholewheat shortbread biscuits.

Chapter 7

How to Assess and Plan your Diet

By now you must be fully aware that there is a strong link between diet and health. The fact that so many people are seriously concerned about this prompted us to devise nutrition tables which could be used as a 'ready reckoner' for assessing and planning diets. Essentially, the tables in Chapter 8 give the nutritional value of food portions. This means that you can evaluate your diet without having to weigh your food.

What's in the tables?

1 Foods are listed alphabetically so you can easily find them in the tables.

2 A brief description of the food is given to help you match your food with the appropriate item in the tables.

3 A code is positioned directly above each food item indicating if it contains added salt or sugar. This is useful if you are concerned about reducing your intake of these items.

4 The weight (or volume in the case of alcoholic drinks) and a description of the food portion are given. This is useful if your food portion differs significantly from the one presented.

5 For each food portion the amounts of energy, fat and dietary fibre are given. The energy values will be of interest to those of you trying to reduce your energy intake. The fat values will be important to those of you wishing to cut down on the amount of fat in your diet. This may be necessary for specific health reasons or

simply to comply with healthy eating guidelines. The figures for dietary fibre will be useful for individuals who have been advised to increase their intake of fibre. This could be to relieve constipation or to comply with NACNE recommendations.

6 The alcohol content of alcoholic drinks is given. This is useful for following the guidelines of recent medical reports.

7 Nutrients found in the specified food portions in useful amounts are given. All the nutrients quoted in the tables provide at least one-tenth of the recommended daily amount (RDA) for men in the eighteen to thirty-four age range with sedentary occupations. This information will enable you to see at a glance if major nutrients are generally represented in your meals. Food portions providing half or more of the RDA are marked with an asterisk. Some people have special needs for specific nutrients: for example, extra iron for the expectant mother, vitamin D for the housebound and vitamin C after an injury or major surgery. Individuals with these issues in mind will find this part of the tables particularly helpful.

How the tables were compiled

A great deal of discussion took place before a method for estimating the size of food portions was agreed. The whole question of food portions is highly controversial. Nutritionists argue amongst themselves about this and it is unlikely that there will ever be universal agreement about what constitutes a 'standard' or 'average' portion. The food portions used in these tables are considered as estimates and should be interpreted as such.

Estimating the size of food portions Foods were purchased and either used as such or made up according to standard recipes quoted in Tables of Food Composition. To estimate portion size three different people were asked independently to serve what they considered to be a small, medium and large portion.

Appropriate serving vessels were selected for this procedure: for example, dinner plates, soup bowls, mugs, and the scales used were accurate to the nearest gram. For each food item there were nine weights: that is three small, three medium and three large. The mean value of the medium-size portion was used in the tables. So when you interpret the tables remember the portions are 'middle of the road' relative to large and small. When foods purchased were already in the form of a unit such as one pork chop, one brown roll, one jam doughnut, three different brands were used and the mean value taken as the weight of the item. This weight was either used as it was or in multiples depending on the agreed medium-size portion estimated as previously described.

The nutritional analysis of food portions The nutritional analysis of the food portions can be considered under three headings:

1 *Added salt and sugar* – The presence of added salt and sugar, was determined by referring to (a) manufacture of food products, (b) food labels, (c) standard recipe formulations and (d) standard food preparation procedures.

2 *Nutrients* – Once the weight of the food portion was estimated the nutritional value was calculated using Tables of Food Composition. The nutrients presented relate specifically to NACNE and COMA recommendations, RDAs and in the case of alcohol Royal College medical reports.

3 *Nutrition biased statements* – These were made to highlight 'healthy eating' issues and were essential when food tables failed to give basic figures for the newer 'healthier' varieties of food products.

How to use the tables

First decide what it is you want to know. The tables can be used for lots of different reasons so it is important that you establish at the outset your particular requirements. You may be interested in some or all of the following.

· Which foods contain *added salt and sugar*
· The *energy* value of food portions
· The amount of *fat* in food portions
· The amount of *dietary fibre* in food portions
· The *alcohol* content of alcoholic drinks
· Food portions providing *nutrients* in useful amounts

Looking foods up in the tables It is worth turning the pages of the tables a few times to get the general flavour before you use them. The more you use the tables the easier it will become for you to find what you are looking for. Food items have deliberately been kept separate to allow for flexibility of different combinations of food. For example, when looking up a cup of tea with sugar and milk you will need to look up the three items separately.

You may find that the tables don't always include the food you are looking for. You can deal with this in two ways. Either scrutinize the tables and find what you consider to be the nearest equivalent food and use that set of figures, or read food labels and use any nutritional information presented (p.44).

How to assess your diet

1 *Record your food intake* – Take a double sheet of A4 paper and mark it out as shown in Table 7.1. Using the record sheet write down everything you eat and drink for one whole day. Ensure that you describe your foods as accurately as possible. For example 'meat' would be inadequate; you would need to say what kind of meat and whether or not the fat was eaten.

2 *Record the relevant nutritional information* – At the end of the day look up each food item in the tables and record the facts that you are interested in.

Table 7.1 Nutrition profile

Description of food portion	Sa (√)	Su (√)	En (kcal)	Fat (g)	Fib (g)	Alc (g)	Nutrients (√)								
							Pro	Ca	Fe	A	D	B_1	B_2	B_3	C
Daily totals															

For *added salt and sugar* in food place a tick in the relevant columns.

For *energy, fat, fibre and alcohol* record the figures in the relevant columns.

For *nutrients found in useful amounts* place a tick in the relevant columns.

3 *Evaluate your diet* – For foods containing *added salt and sugar* look through the tables to find out if there are alternative foods to replace those with these added ingredients.

For *energy, fat, fibre and alcohol* add up the daily totals. For energy intake refer to your RDA as a general guide. Your energy intake for weight reduction should be around 1000kcal and containing not less than 800 kcal. Your fat intake should not exceed 87g. For dietary fibre aim at getting 30g, and for alcohol, on the assumption that you spread your target allowance over a week, intake should not exceed 16g for women and 24g for men. If you have alcohol-free days you can vary this (p.84).

For the presence of *nutrients in useful amounts* examine meals separately, i.e. breakfast, midday and evening meals. At each of these meals aim to have all the major nutrients represented with the exception of vitamin D (see Table 3.1). This particular vitamin is controversial and as a very general guide it may be prudent to ensure its presence about once a day. You may find this difficult because vitamin D is not widely distributed in foods. The tables show that eggs, oily fish and certain breakfast cereals are useful sources and so are foods in which margarine is used as an ingredient because this fat is fortified with vitamin D.

The next step Having assessed your diet you may now possibly feel satisfied that all is well or you may decide it is necessary to bring about some changes. To change the diet of a lifetime is not easy, and eating habits are not changed overnight. The record of your food intake is a good place to begin because it will represent your usual choice of food and you can use the tables to deviate from this.

Tips for planning and changing your diet

This section points out practical ways of achieving a healthy eating pattern. An attempt has been made to draw attention to the relevant nutritional background so that you can understand the reasons behind the suggested measures.

To reduce your intake of added salt Salt finds its way into the foods we eat by different routes. The most obvious way is by adding salt when the food is served. You will note from the tables that many foods have added salt before the food is served. There are several reasons for this. Salt is frequently used in basic cooking processes such as the boiling of foods like rice, pasta and vegetables. Many standard recipes include salt as an ingredient, even sweet dishes sometimes have salt included. Salt is added to many food products when they are being manufactured and this can be detected by reading food labels. For example, added salt is found in foods such as biscuits, breakfast cereals, canned vegetables and in sweets. Salt is also used in the production of foods such as cheese, butter, margarine and low-fat spread, bacon, kippers, bread and pasta. Therefore when you eat these foods you are eating added salt.

Choosing food to reduce salt intake

- Read food labels carefully and opt for foods 'without added salt' rather than with added salt.
- Look out for the word 'brine'; it is worth remembering that pickled gherkins and olives are often sold in brine (solution of salt and water). Canned pulses such as red kidney beans, and vegetables in general, are frequently in brine. Go for alternatives if at all possible. Consider using dried pulses and fresh vegetables so that salt can be left out altogether.
- Restrict the amount of 'salty' snacks you eat – such as roasted salted nuts and crisps. Choose unsalted nuts and go for the crisps with the bag of salt but don't 'salt and shake'.

- When choosing foods such as butter and low-fat spreads go for the unsalted varieties.
- Restrict your intake of foods that have been preserved with salt such as bacon and kippers.

Preparing food to reduce salt intake

- Although it is customary to add approximately a teaspoon (5ml) of salt to one litre of water when boiling vegetables, rice and pasta, ask yourself 'Is this practice really necessary?' Try cooking without salt and find out for yourself. If cooked properly these foods taste quite delicious in their own right. The use of fresh herbs can enhance the flavour of vegetables enormously. For example, fresh mint in peas and potatoes and basil in tomato dishes. Savoury rice dishes can be 'spiced up' to have exciting colours and flavours. Saffron is perhaps rather expensive for this but turmeric is an economical alternative. Generous sprinklings of freshly chopped herbs on any of these foods will add to the taste and appearance. Forget the single sprig of parsley that so often looks limp and weary. Sprinkle the herb with a heavy hand so that you can appreciate its taste.
- When following recipes seriously question the inclusion of salt as an essential ingredient. Salt can be left out of many recipe formulations without devastating results. Phrases such as 'add a pinch of salt', 'add salt to taste' and 'adjust seasoning' should be viewed with caution. Remember that other ingredients in the recipe will have characteristic flavours of their own and these can be enhanced by imaginative use of flavourings other than salt.
- When adding flavourings to foods such as soups, sauces and casseroles beware of the flavoured salts. Garlic and celery salt, for example, are salt-based flavourings. Better to use fresh garlic and invest in a garlic press; or a stick of celery which you can quickly chop.
- In recipes stipulating the use of fat such as butter use the slightly salted or unsalted varieties. However, these fats are not as yellow

in colour as the salted counterparts so the colour of certain products for example shortbread and pastry may be less golden when cooked.

- If you have to use foods canned in brine simply put the food in a sieve and wash the brine away under the cold water tap.
- If you only have salted nuts wash the salt away as for foods canned in brine.
- When preserving foods choose methods that avoid the use of salt, the process of salting vegetables being an absolute taboo. If possible freeze your surplus foods.

Serving food to reduce salt intake

- Throw away your salt cellar! Well, certainly get out of the habit of putting it on the meal table. The seemingly unobtrusive sprinkling of salt on your food or the very obvious little heap at the edge of the plate are both habits you should try to break.
- You can use a salt substitute in place of salt. These are low-sodium and high-potassium salts. But, in the long term, it may be prudent to lose your 'salt appetite' and the use of these substitutes will not help in this process.

To reduce your intake of added sugar 'Sugar, sugar everywhere': yes, almost, and it is easy to understand why this is so when you look at the myriad functions of sugar in food products. Sugar is used as a flavouring, a tenderizer in baked products, in the aeration of creamed cakes, to aid moisture retention in cakes, it contributes to the browning of baked products, it is used to activate yeast, as a stabilizer in egg-white foams, it reduces the risk of curdling in custards, it affects the texture of starch-based sauces and puddings, it is used as a preservative, and to coat foods as sugar or as a syrup, and it is the main ingredient of icings and sweets.

Sometimes the presence of sugar in foods is obvious because they are sweet. However, it may be less obvious and when this is the case nutritionists refer to the sugar as 'hidden sugar'. Food labels will show if sugar has been used in the product but many people need to increase their vocabulary if efficiency is to be achieved in spotting the presence of this little demon! Look out for words like 'sugar' certainly and don't let descriptions such as brown, muscovado, natural, raw, raw cane and cane-unrefined mislead you. Remember that the following are all types of sugar: cane syrup, corn syrup, dextrose, glucose syrup, honey, invert sugar syrup, lactose, molasses, sucrose, malt extract, malt syrup, maple syrup. It is important that you familiarize yourself with this terminology. You will obviously expect certain foods to contain added sugar but it may well come as a big surprise when you discover that certain brands of beefburger, pâté, scampi and high-bake water biscuits also have added sugar.

Choosing food to reduce sugar intake

- Read food labels carefully and opt for foods 'without added sugar' rather than with.
- Be sure to know the different names for sugar and, as well as noting if sugar is present in the food – 'sugar spotting', count up how many times sugar in its various forms is listed in the ingredients. Also note the position of the different forms of sugar on the list remembering that ingredients are listed in order of quantity by weight.
- Don't be lulled into a state of false security by the use of health foods. One particular type of wholemeal digestive biscuit we examined contained cane sugar unrefined, malt, Scottish honey and cane syrup. The supermarket version in contrast contained sugar!
- When choosing breakfast cereals avoid those with sugar coatings.
- When choosing fruit juices go for the unsweetened varieties.
- Choose fresh fruit or fruit canned in its own juice rather than fruit canned in syrup.
- Go for fruit spreads or low-sugar jams rather than jam.
- Remember that coffee whitener is usually made from glucose syrup and vegetable fat.

- Choose starters and main courses at meals and try to get rid of the habit of finishing with a pudding.
- Between-meal snacks such as cakes, buns, biscuits, sweets and chocolate can add substantially to your intake of added sugar. Restrict your intake of these foods. Go for fresh fruit or dried fruit instead. You may well be pleased that plain chocolate, certain sweets, cakes and puddings provide iron in useful amounts. Keep this in perspective and do not use this as an excuse to eat such foods!

Preparing food to reduce sugar intake

- 'Convenience food' sauces frequently contain added sugar. Think really carefully about this. Consider preparing your own sauces bearing in mind that kitchen aids such as a blender, food processor and microwave oven and 'all-in-one' methods of sauce making can save a lot of time. Perhaps the healthier version of the recipe might not be so difficult to achieve?
- When making cakes and puddings make more use of ingredients such as dried fruit, bananas, carrots and sweet potatoes. Use these ingredients as a replacement or to reduce the amount of sugar in the recipe: e.g. sugar, honey, black treacle and golden syrup. Don't just improvise; find appropriate recipes for this purpose. There are plenty of books available with good recipes.
- Seriously question the use of sugar as an ingredient in recipes. Sometimes it is totally unnecessary. For example, salad dressings can be stabilized with ingredients such as mustard and pepper; chilli-con-carne does not, as some recipes suggest, require the addition of sugar; fresh fruit salad steeped in the fruits' own juices or with added unsweetened fruit juice is a pleasant contrast to fruit soaked in sugar syrup. Also sweet and sour dishes can be adequately sweetened by using ingredients such as carrot and pineapple.
- As a change from preserving your glut of fruit by jam making why not make fruit purées and freeze these in handy portions for later use? Alternatively make low-sugar jam.

Serving food to reduce sugar intake

- If you are used to adding sugar or honey to beverages try to get out of this habit. Use sweeteners if you really must but in the long term it would be better if you could go without and lose your 'sweet tooth'.
- The practice of sprinkling sugar onto breakfast cereals or adding honey is also best left behind. Dried fruit (intact if small or chopped if large) is an interesting alternative. Some fresh fruits such as apples and bananas blend in well with certain breakfast cereals.
- When serving fresh fruit enjoy the natural flavours. Try to avoid the sprinkling of sugar.
- If puddings are on the menu remember that additions such as Dream Topping, condensed milk, custard and some types of aerosol cream contain added sugar.

To reduce your intake of energy By now you must be fully aware that the energy values of different foods vary enormously. Whether you are reducing your energy intake to comply with RDAs or targets in weight reduction programmes it is important that the loss of calories is not at the expense of other nutrients. To ensure a healthy eating pattern follow the tips for planning and changing your diet (p.70). Be sure that you distribute your food intake as evenly as possible throughout the day.

To reduce your intake of fat Some foods obviously contain fat and if this is the case nutritionists use the term 'visible fat'. Visible fats are easy to identify and include the fat on meat, butter, margarine, cream and oils. Fats that are not obviously present in foods are described as 'invisible fats' and include the fat present in lean meat which is referred to as marbling, fat in egg yolk and the fat in pastries, cakes and biscuits.

When the function of fat in food preparation is considered it is easy to understand why fat finds its way into so many of our foods.

It is used in creamed cake mixtures as a means of incorporating air, as a shortening agent in biscuits, pastries and cakes; to produce the characteristic flakes in flaky pastry; to keep cakes and bread moist; to stop flour-based sauces from being lumpy; in salad dressings; to add colour to food; as a glaze for basting when grilling or roasting; as a cooking medium for frying and also for greasing to stop foods from sticking to cooking vessels.

You will note that the tables refer to the quantity of fat in food or what nutritionists refer to as *total fat.* You may also be interested to know about the quality or type of fat. This is highly relevant because healthy eating guidelines suggest a reduction in the amount of saturated fat with some of this being replaced with polyunsaturated fat. Polyunsaturated fats and oils are widely available so it is sensible to use these as a replacement whenever possible.

Choosing food to reduce fat intake In view of the different sources of fat in the diet and their contribution to fat intake as a whole this section focuses on food commodities.

Meat Approximately 25 per cent of the fat in the diet comes from meat (bacon, beef, lamb, pork, veal, poultry, offal, sausages and products made from these foods). So it is very important to reduce your intake of fat from this source. There are lots of ways in which this can be achieved.

- Choose lean cuts of meat in preference to fatty meat.
- Choose 'quality' mince rather than fatty mince or better still buy some lean stewing steak and make your own mince.
- Go for lean bacon rashers rather than streaky.
- Choose sausages with reduced fat content in preference to full-fat varieties.
- Choose meat products which do not include pastry.
- Meat curries are generally high in fat so go steady here; better to opt for the drier tikka and tandoori dishes.
- When choosing poultry select chicken and turkey rather than goose or duck.

- Choose the light meat of poultry in preference to the dark meat. The light meat contains less fat than the dark meat. In roast chicken the light meat is about 4 per cent fat and the dark meat 7 per cent fat: in roast turkey the light meat is 1 per cent fat and the dark meat 4 per cent fat.

Butter and margarine About 24 per cent of the fat in the diet comes from butter and margarine. Together with meat this is the most important area to look at for reducing the total fat in your diet.

- Choose low-fat spreads in place of butter and margarine. This will be fine for spreads and jacket potatoes. However, you will need specially adapted recipes available from manufacturers if you intend using these fats in food preparation. This is because low-fat spreads have a high water content which interferes with the usual function of fats in recipes.

Milk Approximately 12 per cent of the fat in the diet comes from whole milk.

- Choose the semi-skimmed or skimmed varieties which contain less fat than whole milk. The legal minimum fat content of whole milk is 3 per cent, semi-skilled milk is between 1.5 and 1.8 per cent fat and skimmed milk is less than 0.3 per cent fat.

Cheese Approximately 5 per cent of the fat in the diet comes from cheese.

- Be aware of the different fat contents of cheese and choose those with the lower amount of fat. Edam contains less fat than cheddar: the former is 23 per cent fat and the latter 34 per cent. Similarly choose between cottage and cream cheese; these have fat contents of 4 per cent and 47 per cent respectively.
- Try the low-fat range of cheeses which contain about half the fat of their full-fat counterparts.
- Choose really strong-flavoured cheeses such as parmesan or 'extra' mature cheddar so you can use less as flavourings in recipes.

Cream Cream accounts for about 2 per cent of the fat in the diet.

· To reduce fat from this source go for Dream Topping in place of cream or try quark or low-fat yogurt instead.
· Remember the different fat contents of cream and use this as a guide when choosing cream (Table 7.2).

Table 7.2 The fat content of cream

Type of cream	Percentage fat
Clotted cream	55
Double cream	48
Extra-thick double cream	48
Whipped cream	35
Whipping cream	35
Aerosol cream	35
'Spooning' or extra-thick textured cream	30
Sterilized cream	23
Single cream	18
Soured cream	18
Half cream	12

Cakes, pastries and biscuits About 6 per cent of the fat in the diet comes from cakes, pastries and biscuits.
· Cut down on your intake of these food products. To satisfy your desire for sweetness use fresh or dried fruit.
· Choose cakes and buns which are not high in fat content. Look through the tables and select buns or sweetened breads, scones and certain cakes, for example Jaffa cakes and sponge cakes with a jam filling.

Other tips
· Go easy on your intake of savoury snacks such as crisps and roasted salted nuts. Choose crisps with reduced fat content in preference to full-fat varieties.

- Choose low-calorie sauces and dressings in preference to traditional ones.
- Choose pulses such as red kidney beans and baked beans from time to time in your meal planning schemes as a change from meat, fish, eggs and cheese.
- If you really must have chips use the low-fat varieties which usually contain about 30 per cent less fat than ordinary chips.
- Choose foods that have been grilled rather than fried.

Preparing food to reduce fat intake

- When preparing meat or poultry remove the visible fat. In the case of poultry you will need to remove the skin because the fat is attached to it.
- When meat dishes have been cooked remove any visible fat that floats to the surface. This can be done by one of three methods: (1) wipe the surface with absorbent paper; (2) spoon the fat off and (3) let the food cool and remove the fat when it has solidified.
- Prepare sauces that are non-fat based. That is, avoid those made from fat and flour or cream. Try vegetable-based sauces such as tomato and use cornflour as a means of thickening. You can cut down on the fat content of fat/flour sauces by using skimmed milk.
- Prepare salad dressings from low-fat yogurt for a change. Salad dressings can add considerably to fat intake.
- When cooking with cheese use the low-fat varieties or less than specified if strong-flavoured cheeses are chosen.
- Use semi-skimmed or skimmed milk whenever possible in place of whole milk, e.g. in milky drinks and pancakes.
- Try using alternatives to cream in recipes. Yogurt can be used as a substitute in cheesecakes, dips and as a garnish to goulash. Dream Topping can reduce the fat content of that old favourite sherry trifle.
- Seriously question the use of pastry. This can add lots of fat to your diet. If you are using pastry it is better to go for shortcrust

rather than flaky. The former is about 32 per cent fat and the latter 41 per cent.

- Read recipes critically and question the role of fat in the dish. In some recipes you can reduce the amount of fat used or even omit it altogether without disastrous results. For example, in the preliminary frying of mince for Bolognese sauce why not omit the fat and use a non-stick pan? When making hummus (chickpeas, tahini, olive oil, garlic, lemon juice) try leaving out the olive oil.
- As far as possible grill instead of fry. If frying is a must, follow the guidelines below.

To reduce the amount of fat in fried food

- Cook the food at the recommended temperature for frying as food absorbs fat at low temperatures. It is worth investing in a frying thermometer if this method of cooking is one you will find hard to drop.
- Apart from starchy foods such as chips or doughnuts coat foods to be fried in batter or egg and crumbs: these coatings form a seal around the food and prevent fat absorption during cooking.
- Avoid turning burgers and rissoles excessively during cooking and ensure food mixtures to be fried are firmly intact before frying. Once these foods break up fat will get into every little crevice.
- Immediately after frying wipe the food with absorbent paper to remove any surface fat.

Serving food to reduce fat intake

- The good old knob of butter on vegetables is something you should try to live without! Why not sprinkle some freshly chopped herbs over your food instead.
- Jacket potatoes can be served with low-fat yogurt dressing rather than sour cream or butter.
- Soups can be served with a whirl of low-fat yogurt instead of cream.
- Try eating bread and crispbread without any fat. If you have interesting toppings the fat will not be missed. Alternatively

spread the fat very thinly and use low-fat spread instead of butter or margarine. Why not simply fail to put the butter out? Out of sight out of mind.

· Go steady on the amount of fat-based sauces and salad dressings that you serve. Have enough to taste rather than flood your plate.
· If the meat on your plate has any visible fat just cut it off and don't eat it.

To increase your intake of dietary fibre Dietary fibre is found in foods of plant origin only. Do not be confused by the term muscle-fibre as found in meat and fish; these fibres are entirely different. Since dietary fibre comes from plants it is not surprising that vegans (people who eat plant foods only) have higher than average intakes of fibre. However, not all of us want to make such dramatic changes to our diet. The following guidelines show that there are lots of things you can do to increase your intake of fibre within the framework of an omnivorous (meat eating) diet.

Choosing food to increase fibre intake

· Choose wholewheat bread in preference to white bread.
· Choose wholemeal pasta rather than the white or flavoured varieties.
· Choose brown rice rather than white rice.
· Choose breakfast cereals with the fibre content in mind. If you look at the tables you will see which ones are best.
· Go for crispbreads, preferably the high-fibre varieties, and oat-cakes rather than crackers.
· At meal times always include a cereal food – preferably unrefined as described above.
· Read food labels and look for 'high-fibre' varieties, for example wholewheat spaghetti canned in tomato sauce.
· As a change from meat, fish, cheese and eggs base your meals on pulses, for example baked beans, dahl, red kidney beans. Go for mixtures such as chilli-con-carne so that you get the best of both

worlds. Similarly include nuts as a basis for meals.

- Have more meals based on bread.
- Be sure to include fruit and vegetables in your meals – preferably fresh. Remember that the skins are useful sources of fibre so choose jacket potatoes rather than boiled. Berry fruits such as raspberries are higher in fibre than other types of fruit so choose these when you can.
- If you feel a craving for something sweet between meals choose fresh or dried fruit rather than sweets and chocolate. Look at the tables to see which cakes, pastries, scones and buns have the most fibre and choose these rather than the fibre-depleted kinds. All-Bran loaf is high in fibre.
- If puddings are a must, although, hopefully, you will learn to live without them, choose fresh fruit salad or fruit canned in its own juice. Look at the tables to see which puddings give the most fibre. Bread pudding is a useful source of fibre.

Preparing food to increase fibre intake

- When preparing dishes based on pasta and rice use the unrefined varieties. But remember that as a rule wholemeal pasta and brown rice take longer to cook than their refined counterparts.
- Make use of bread, preferably wholemeal or brown, in food preparation. It can be used for toppings, coatings, fillers in burger and loaf mixtures, stuffings, soups, sauces and puddings.
- Remember that breakfast cereals can be used in many exciting ways in recipes. They are a good way of bridging the 'fibre-gap'. If you aren't too keen on eating them in the traditional style consider using them as coatings, toppings, fillers in burgers and meat loaves and in cakes.
- When preparing dishes where flour is an ingredient use wholemeal rather than white. The former contains 8.6g of fibre per 100g and the latter 3.6g per 100g. This may sound silly, but if your recipe tells you to sift the flour don't forget to tip the bran remaining in the sieve in with the rest of the flour!

- Peel vegetables only when necessary. The skins on potatoes for example not only add fibre but the flavour is more pronounced and less vitamin C is lost during cooking. Also nutrients found concentrated just under the skin such as protein and minerals are not lost. You will, however, have to rationalize 'to peel or not to peel' because in some circumstances it is probably better to peel. For instance the curled up papery skins of a tomato add nothing to the palatability or aesthetics of lasagne or ratatouille!
- When making sauces based on fat and flour use wholewheat flour but remember the sauce will not be smooth or white. Make breadsauce using wholewheat bread and prepare this sauce for dishes other than roast chicken. It goes well with sausages, bacon and the different types of bean and nut loaves. Vegetable purées can be used as a change from traditional sauces.
- When making soups using vegetables as the main ingredient leave the chunky vegetables intact or liquidize. Do not push the mixture through a sieve because you will lose much of the fibre.
- When preparing fruit – only peel when necessary but as in the case of vegetables keep this in perspective.

Serving food to increase fibre intake

- Serve bread with meals.
- Serve side salads with main meals (unless the meal is a salad).
- Have a bowl of fresh fruit on the table to tempt people to eat it as a pudding.
- Serve toasted wholewheat croutons to be sprinkled over food, e.g. macaroni, salad, soups.
- Sprinkle bran or wheatgerm over your breakfast cereal.

To reduce your intake of alcohol. Alcoholic beverages can easily creep into your eating pattern. This is not surprising given the pervasiveness of alcohol in our society and its social importance.

Men and women have different capacities for coping with alcohol, because of differences in body composition. Women have more fat and less water in their bodies than men and as a result the alcohol is more concentrated and stays in the body cells of women for longer. Because of this men and women have different limits for safe drinking.

You may have come across the idea of monitoring alcohol intake by using a unit system whereby one unit is equal to a glass of wine, a measure of a spirit or a half-pint of beer. This is the equivalent of 8g of alcohol. It is generally agreed that women should not exceed 14 units and men 21 units a week. Within this scheme hazardous drinking has been defined as between 14 and 35 units for women and between 21 and 50 units for men. The unit system is fine, but for greater accuracy, we have given grams of alcohol in the tables. On this basis *women should observe an upper limit of 112g and men 168g of alcohol per week.*

Your weekly guide to reduce alcohol intake

- Try to have at least two days in the week designated as 'alcohol free'. Have some refreshing alternatives to alcoholic drinks to compensate.
- Try to avoid drinking on your own. This may be difficult if you have had a hard day or are feeling low; but it will be to your advantage if you can manage to resist the temptation.
- At the pub, wine bar or club – that is when you are drinking socially – it would be better if you did not join in rounds. People seem to get through much more drink in this kind of situation.
- If you are celebrating or partying set yourself an upper limit of drinks beforehand and keep to it.
- Whenever you drink alcoholic beverages alternate with a non-alcoholic one.
- When you get that 'I'm dying for a drink' feeling remember the cost and the calories. If you don't drink you will save money and additional calories.
- The tables show that some alcoholic drinks make a significant contribution to the intake of certain nutrients: for example, iron in red wine and cider and B-vitamins in beers. Keep this in perspective, regard this as a bonus and not an excuse to drink!

Figure 7.1 Meal-planning scheme

Group	Examples
A	Bread, Pasta, Rice, Breakfast cereals, Crispbread
B	Fruit, Vegetables, Fruit juices
C	Meat, Poultry, Offal, Fish, Milk, Cheese, Yogurt, Eggs, Pulses, Nuts
D	Sugar, Jam, Soft drinks, Puddings, Sweets, Chocolate, Cakes, Pastries
E	Butter, Margarine, Cream, Fried foods, Pastry products, Salad dressing
F	Salt, Foods canned in brine, Salted foods, Salt flavourings
G	Beer, Cider, Sherry, Port, Wine, Lager, Liqueurs, Spirits

Choose foods from the A B C groups
Restrict foods from the D E F G groups

To ensure representation of the major nutrients One golden rule: 'plan your meals around foods and not nutrients'. This is important because we eat foods, not nutrients. To ensure a healthy mixture of foods, select foods from the A B and C groups (Figure 7.1). This will mean that cereals, preferably unrefined; fruit or vegetables; and any one or more of the following: meat, fish, eggs, milk, cheese, yogurt, pulses and nuts will be represented. In the interest of health you are strongly advised to restrict your intake of the foods in the groups D E F and G, that is, sugar, fat, salt and alcohol.

If you are concerned about your intake of a particular nutrient you can scrutinize the tables to identify foods providing it. Look for food portions showing an asterisk above the nutrient as these are rich sources. The expectant mother would be advised to look at the section on offal if she is worried about her intake of iron. The housebound person would be wise to find foods with useful amounts of vitamin D and might select breakfast cereals fortified with this nutrient, eggs and egg dishes and oily fish. Margarine and low-fat spreads contain more vitamin D than butter. Although this does not show in the food portions it would be sensible to use margarine or low-fat spread instead of butter.

Meals have been focused on deliberately to ensure that a mixture of foods is eaten at a given time. This is very important because various nutrients interact with each other so that the body can use them efficiently. If certain nutrients are not consumed at the same time the body will not be able to utilize them properly. This will be clear from the following examples.

1 Vitamin C is needed for the absorption of non-haem iron; that is the iron from non-meat sources.
2 Carbohydrates have a 'protein-sparing' function. If the food lacks carbohydrate more protein than usual will be used as an energy source.
3 When pulses or nuts are the focal point of meals it is essential to eat cereal foods to ensure that the quality of protein is enhanced.

With all of this in mind you may well be asking what about the nutrients in 'between-meal snacks'? Simply, the value in nutritional terms depends upon the mixture in question. A portion of dried figs contains a useful amount of iron but unless you have something like fruit juice, for example, containing vitamin C the iron will not be absorbed efficiently. A portion of peanuts may provide a useful amount of protein but unless a cereal food is eaten with it the quality of the protein will not be as good.

In the interest of health it is advisable to distribute your food intake throughout the day. Aim to have breakfast, a midday meal and an evening meal. No breakfast, the 'bitty' lunch and the big meal at the end of the day should be bygones. Nutritionists have differences of opinion about lots of things but this is something on which there is general agreement.

Table 7.3 Nutrition profile – before

Description of food portion	Sa (√)	Su (√)	En (kcal)	Fat (g)	Fib (g)	Alc (g)	Nutrients (√)								
							Pro	Ca	Fe	A	D	B_1	B_2	B_3	C
sweetened orange juice		✓	100									✓			✓
white toast with butter and marmalade	✓	✓	335	13	3			✓	✓			✓		✓	
2 cups tea with milk			54	2											
1 danish pastry	✓	✓	375	18	3			✓	✓			✓		✓	
1 cup instant coffee with milk			27	1											
6 cream crackers with butter & cheddar cheese	✓		620	44	2		✓	✓		✓			✓	✓	
2 chocolate biscuits	✓	✓	260	14	2										
1 cup instant coffee with milk			27	1											
1 Mars bar	✓	✓	285	12				✓							
1 cup tea with milk			27	1											
rock salmon in batter (chipshop)	✓		545	39	1		✓	✓	✓			✓	✓	✓	
1 portion chips with tomato ketchup	✓	✓	690	29			✓		✓			✓		✓	✓
Instant dessert	✓	✓	100	6				✓							
1 cup tea with milk			27	1											
2 pints beer			360			36		✓					✓	✓	
1 packet salted peanuts	✓		145	12	2									✓	
Daily totals	9	7	3977	193	13	36									

Table 7.4 Nutrition profile – after

Description of food portion	Sa (√)	Su (√)	En (kcal)	Fat (g)	Fib (g)	Alc (g)	Nutrients (√)								
							Pro	Ca	Fe	A	D	B_1	B_2	B_3	C
unsweetened orange juice			65						√			√			√
boiled egg with brown toast & low-fat spread	√		305	14	4		√	√	√	√	√	√	√	√	
2 cups tea with semi-skimmed milk			34	2											
sponge cake, jam-filled	√	√	105	2											
1 cup instant coffee with milk			27	1											
6 pieces crispbread with edam cheese	√		390	20	6		√	√		√			√	√	
1 slice all-bran loaf	√	√	205	1	4			√	√			√	√	√	
1 banana and 1 apple			105		5										√
1 cup instant coffee with milk			27	1											
1 cup tea with milk			27	1											
2 grilled cod steaks with cheese sauce	√		285	14			√	√		√		√	√	√	
jacket potato and carrots			157	6					√	√		√		√	√
wholewheat roll	√		135	2	5				√			√		√	
fresh fruit salad			100		4										√
1 cup tea with semi-skimmed milk			17	1											
1 pint beer			180			18		√					√	√	
Daily totals	6	2	2164	59	34	18									

Sample analysis Table 7.3 shows a sample record of food intake for one whole day. After reading it carefully to see how you might improve upon it, look at Table 7.4 and the following commentary.

Comments on nutrition profiles – before and after

- Added salt – Reduced from 12 food items to 7.
- Added sugar – Reduced from 7 food items to 2.
- Energy – Reduced from 3977 kcal to 2164 kcal.
- Fat – Reduced from 193g to 59g.
- Fibre – Raised from 13g to 34g.
- Alcohol – Reduced from 36g to 18g.
- Nutrients
  Breakfast – Improved to include the missing protein, vitamin A and vitamin B_2.
  Midday meal – Improved to include the missing iron, vitamin B_1 and vitamin C.
  Evening meal – Improved to include the missing vitamin A.
  Vitamin D present in one meal, i.e. breakfast.

Conclusion – Generally a reduction in the amount of foods consumed containing added *salt* and added *sugar*. Energy intake in accord with RDA. *Fat* intake below COMA maximum of 87g/day. *Fibre* intake just over NACNE recommendation of 30g/day. *Alcohol* intake – fine if alcohol-free days are planned during the week. *Nutrients* represented at each meal and vitamin D in one meal.

You will no doubt realize that dietary change can be effected in many different ways. You may not like the suggestions made, and it is up to you to make your own changes. It's your diet, your food, your choice. Use the tables to suit your own particular likes and dislikes and your philosophy.

Chapter 8

Food Composition Tables

Key to tables

Sa	=	Added salt
Su	=	Added sugar *Note* the definition of the word 'sugar' is contentious (see p.73 for details).
En(kcal)	=	Energy in kcal 1–20 to nearest 1g 21+ to nearest 5g
Fat(g)	=	Total fat in grams to nearest 1g
Fib(g)	=	Dietary fibre in grams to nearest 1g
Alc(g)	=	Alcohol in grams to nearest 1g

(Quantities of the above are all rounded up.)

Nutrients	=	Nutrients present in useful amounts providing at least 1/10 RDA for men 18–34 age range, with sedentary occupations
*	=	Rich sources of nutrients providing at least 1/2 RDA for men 18–34 age range, with sedentary occupations
Pro	=	Protein
Ca	=	Calcium
Fe	=	Iron
A	=	Vitamin A, retinol equivalents
D	=	Vitamin D, cholecalciferol
B_1	=	Vitamin B_1, thiamine
B_2	=	Vitamin B_2, riboflavin
B_3	=	Vitamin B_3 nicotinic acid equivalents
C	=	Vitamin C, ascorbic acid
na	=	No available figures

Table 8.1 Alcoholic beverages

Food, and portion	Vol (ml)	En (kcal)	Fat (g)	Fib (g)	Alc (g)	Nutrients
All figures presented are based on pub measures						
Beer						
Brown ale bottled, 1 bottle	275	75	0	0	6	
Draught bitter, 1 pint	568	180	0	0	18	Ca/$B_{2,3}$
mild, 1 pint	568	140	0	0	15	Ca/$B_{2,3}$
Keg bitter, 1 pint	568	175	0	0	17	$B_{2,3}$
Lager bottled, 1 bottle	275	80	0	0	9	
Pale ale bottled, 1 bottle	275	90	0	0	9	
Stout bottled, 1 bottle	275	100	0	0	8	
Cider						
Dry, 1 pint	568	205	0	0	22	Fe
Sweet, 1 pint	568	240	0	0	21	Fe
Wine						
Red wine, 4fl oz	114	80	0	0	11	Fe
Rose, 4fl oz	114	80	0	0	10	Fe
White wine, dry 4fl oz	114	75	0	0	10	
White wine, sparkling, 4fl oz	114	85	0	0	11	
White wine, sweet, 4fl oz	114	105	0	0	12	
Wine – fortified						
Port, ⅓ gill	47	75	0	0	7	
Sherry dry, ⅓ gill	47	55	0	0	7	
Sherry medium, ⅓ gill	47	55	0	0	7	
Sherry sweet, ⅓ gill	47	65	0	0	7	
Vermouths						
Dry vermouth, ⅓ gill	47	55	0	0	7	
Sweet vermouth, ⅓ gill	47	70	0	0	6	
Liqueurs, ⅙ gill	24	70	0	0	6	
e.g. cherry brandy and curaçao						
Spirits, ⅙ gill	24	55	0	0	8	
e.g. brandy, gin, rum and whisky						

Table 8.2 Composition of foods

Food, and portion	Wt (g)	En (kcal)	Fat (g)	Fib (g)	Nutrients
Beverages – non-alcoholic Amounts given sufficient for 1 mug/cup					
Bournvita[Sa], 2 heaped tsp	9	35	0	na	
Cocoa, 1 level tsp	3	9	1	na	
Coffee					
ground/infused, cup/mug	195	4	0	na	
powder/granules, 1 heaped tsp	2	2	0	na	
Drinking chocolate[Sa Su], 3 heaped tsp	15	55	1	na	
Horlicks[Sa Su], 4 heaped tsp	20	80	2	na	A/$B_{1,2,3}$
Ovaltine[Su], 4 heaped tsp	15	55	1	na	D/B_1
Tea, infused, cup/mug	195	2	0	na	
Biscuits – plain					
Crackers					
cream crackers[Sa], 3 crackers	21	90	3	1	
wholemeal crackers[Sa Su], 3 crackers	21	85	2	1	
Crispbread, rye[Sa], 3 crispbreads	24	75	1	3	
High fibre crispbreads contain about 30% more fibre					
Matzos, 1 matzo	30	115	1	1	
Oatcakes[Sa Su], 2 oatcakes	26	115	5	1	Fe
Water biscuits[Sa], 3 biscuits	21	90	3	1	
High-bake varieties may contain added sugar					
Biscuits – sweet					
Chocolate biscuits[Sa Su], 1 biscuit	25	130	7	1	
e.g. Penguin and Club biscuits					
Digestive biscuits[Sa Su]					
Chocolate, 2 biscuits	30	150	7	1	
Plain, 2 biscuits	30	140	6	1	

Food, and portion	Wt (g)	En (kcal)	Fat (g)	Fib (g)	Nutrients
Ginger nuts[Sa Su], 2 biscuits	20	90	3	0	
Sandwich biscuits[Sa Su], 2 biscuits	25	130	6	0	
e.g. custard creams, orange creams and bourbon					
Semi-sweet biscuits[Sa Su], 2 biscuits *e.g. Marie, Osborne and rich tea biscuits*	15	70	2	0	
Short-sweet biscuits[Sa Su], 2 biscuits *e.g. shortcake and Lincoln biscuits*	20	95	5	0	
Shortbread[Sa Su], 2 fingers	35	175	9	1	A
Wafers, filled[Sa Su], 3 wafers	18	95	5	0	
Bread and bread rolls – plain					
Breads					
Bread[Sa] – medium sliced from large loaves					
brown, 2 slices	70	155	1	4	Ca/Fe/$B_{1,3}$
white, 2 slices	75	165	1	3	Ca/Fe/$B_{1,3}$
wholemeal, 2 slices	70	150	2	5	Pro/Fe/$B_{1,3}$
Chapatis[Sa], 1 chapati	70	230	9	5	Fe/$B_{1,3}$
made without fat, 1 chapati	70	140	1	4	Fe/$B_{1,3}$
Naan[Sa], 1 naan	170	570	21	4	Pro/Ca*/Fe/A/$B_{1,2,3}$
Papadums[Sa], fried, 2 papadums	22	80	4	2	Fe
Paratha[Sa], 1 paratha	125	405	18	6	Pro/Ca/Fe/A/$B_{1,3}$
Pitta bread[Sa], 1 pitta	65	170	1	3	Ca/Fe/$B_{1,3}$
Wholemeal pitta contains about double the amount of fibre					
Bread rolls					
brown baps[Sa], 1 bap	55	145	2	4	Ca/Fe/$B_{1,3}$
white baps[Sa], 1 bap	55	145	2	2	Ca/Fe/$B_{1,3}$
wholemeal baps[Sa], 1 bap	55	135	2	5	Fe/$B_{1,3}$

Food, and portion	Wt (g)	En (kcal)	Fat (g)	Fib (g)	Nutrients
Bread and buns – sweet					
Breads$^{Sa\ Su}$					
currant bread, 2 slices	50	145	4	2	
malt loaf, 2 medium slices	60	160	1	4	Ca/Fe/$B_{1,3}$
Buns$^{Sa\ Su}$					
Bath bun, 1 bun	55	200	8	1	Ca
Chelsea bun, 1 bun	70	255	10	2	Ca/Fe/$B_{1,3}$
currant bun, 1 bun	50	150	4	1	Ca/B_1
hot cross bun, 1 bun	65	200	4	1	Ca/Fe/B_3
Breakfast cereals					
All-Bran$^{Sa\ Su}$, 1 helping	45	115	2	14	Pro/Fe*/D/$B_{1,}$
Bran, 2 heaped tbsp	6	12	0	2	B_3
Bran Buds$^{Sa\ Su}$, 1 helping	75	205	2	21	Pro/Fe*/D/$B^{*}_{1,}$
Bran Flakes$^{Sa\ Su}$, 1 helping	45	145	1	8	Fe*/D/$B_{1,2,3}$ C*
Coco Pops$^{Sa\ Su}$, 1 helping	35	135	0	0	Fe/$B_{1,2,3}$
Corn Flakes$^{Sa\ Su}$, 1 helping	25	90	0	1	Fe/$B_{1,2,3}$
Crunchy Nut Corn Flakes$^{Sa\ Su}$, 1 helping	45	180	2	1	Fe/D/$B_{1,2,3}$
Frosties$^{Sa\ Su}$, 1 helping	45	170	0	1	Fe/D/$B_{1,2,3}$
Fruit 'n' Fibre$^{Sa\ Su}$, 1 helping	50	175	3	5	Fe/D/$B^{*}_{1,2,3}$
Grapenuts, 1 helping	90	310	0	6	Pro/Fe*/A*/D/
Contains malted barley (see sugar p.73)					$B_{1^*,2^*,3^*}$
Muesli					
Swiss style$^{Sa\ Su}$, 1 helping	95	345	6	8	Pro/Ca/Fe*/$B_{1,}$
extra fruit$^{Sa\ Su}$, 1 helping	95	355	6	5	Pro/Ca/Fe/$B_{2,}$
no added sugar^{Sa}, 1 helping	95	350	8	11	Pro/Fe/$B_{1,2,3}$
Nutri-Grain^{Sa}					
brown rice and rye flakes raisins, 1 helping	60	200	1	6	Fe/D/$B_{1^*,2^*,3^*}$
rye and oat flakes hazelnuts, 1 helping	60	225	6	7	Fe/D/$B_{1^*,2^*,3^*}$

Food, and portion	Wt (g)	En (kcal)	Fat (g)	Fib (g)	Nutrients
wholewheat flakes raisins, 1 helping	60	200	1	7	Fe/D/$B^{*\,*\,*}_{1,\,2,\,3}$
Porridge^{Sa}					
made with milk, 1 helping	160	185	8	1	Pro/Ca/A/$B_{1,\,2,\,3}$
made with milk and water, 1 helping	160	135	5	1	Ca/B_1
made with water, 1 helping	160	80	2	1	
Puffed Wheat, 1 helping	20	65	0	2	
Ready Brek, 1 helping	30	115	3	2	Fe/$B_{1,\,3}$
Contains malt extract (see sugar p.73)					
Rice Krispies$^{Sa\ Su}$, 1 helping	35	130	0	0	Fe/$B_{1,\,2,\,3}$
Ricicles$^{Sa\ Su}$, 1 helping	45	170	0	0	Fe/D/$B_{1,\,2,\,3}$
Shredded Wheat, 2 pieces	45	145	1	5	Fe/$B_{1,\,3}$
Shreddies$^{Sa\ Su}$, 1 helping	55	180	1	6	Fe/$B^{*\,*\,*}_{1,\,2,\,3}$
Special K$^{Sa\ Su}$, 1 helping	35	135	0	1	Fe/$B_{1,\,2,\,3}$
Sugar Puffs^{Su}, 1 helping	50	160	0	2	Fe/B_3
Sultana Bran$^{Sa\ Su}$, 1 helping	35	105	1	5	Fe^{*}/$B_{1,\,2,\,3}$
Weetabix$^{Sa\ Su}$, 2 Weetabix	40	140	1	3	Fe/$B_{1,\,2,\,3}$
Weetaflakes$^{Sa\ Su}$, 1 helping	45	155	1	5	Fe/$B_{2,\,3}$
Wheatgerm, 2 heaped tbsp	15	45	1	2	Fe/B_1
Cakes and pastries					
All-Bran loaf$^{Sa\ Su}$, 1 medium slice	80	205	1	4	Ca/Fe/$B_{1,\,2,\,3}$
Baclava$^{Sa\ Su}$, 1 baclava	110	355	19	2	B_3
Battenburg cake$^{Sa\ Su}$, 1 medium slice	55	205	10	1	
Cheesecake$^{Sa\ Su}$, 1 medium slice	100	410	32	1	Ca/A
Chocolate cake$^{Sa\ Su}$, 1 medium slice with butter icing	40	190	12	1	A/D
Chocolate eclair$^{Sa\ Su}$, 1 eclair	40	150	10	0	A
Cream horn$^{Sa\ Su}$, 1 cream horn	60	260	21	1	A

Food, and portion	Wt (g)	En (kcal)	Fat (g)	Fib (g)	Nutrients
Crispie cakes Sa Su, 2 crispie cakes	30	140	6	0	Fe/$B_{1, 2, 3}$
Croissant Sa Su, 1 croissant	50	180	10	1	Fe/B_3
Custard tart Sa Su, 1 individual	80	220	12	1	Ca/B_1
Danish pastry Sa Su, 1 Danish pastry	100	375	18	3	Ca/Fe/$B_{1, 3}$
Doughnuts Sa Su					
jam filled, 1 doughnut	70	235	10	2	Ca/B_1
ring, 1 doughnut	50	200	11	2	B_1
ring, iced, 1 doughnut	60	230	11	1	B_1
Eccles cake Sa Su, 1 Eccles cake	60	285	16	1	
Flapjacks Sa Su, 1 flapjack	30	145	8	1	
Fondant fancies Sa Su, 1 cake	25	100	4	1	
Fruit cake Sa Su					
plain, 1 medium slice	60	210	8	2	Fe
wholemeal, 1 medium slice	60	220	9	2	Ca/Fe/A
Fruit pie Sa Su, 1 individual	110	405	17	3	Ca/Fe
Gateau Sa Su, 1 medium slice	45	150	8	0	A
Gingerbread Sa Su, 1 medium slice	65	245	8	1	Ca/Fe/A
Jaffa cakes Su, 2 Jaffa cakes	20	75	2	na	
Jam tarts Sa Su, 1 jam tart	35	130	5	1	
Madeira cake Sa Su, 1 medium slice	25	100	4	0	
Meringues Su, 1 meringue filled with fresh cream	35	125	7	0	A
Mince pies Sa Su, 1 individual	50	210	10	1	
Rock cakes Sa Su, 1 cake	80	315	13	1	Ca/A/D
Scotch pancakes Sa Su, 1 pancake	30	90	4	0	
Sponge cake Sa Su					
jam filled, 1 medium slice	35	105	2	0	
with butter icing, 1 medium slice	35	170	11	0	A/D
Swiss roll Su, 1 medium slice	35	95	2	0	

Food, and portion	Wt (g)	En (kcal)	Fat (g)	Fib (g)	Nutrients
chocolate mini[Sa Su], 1 mini roll	25	85	3	1	
Vanilla slice[Sa Su], 1 vanilla slice	75	250	13	1	Ca
Cereal components of meals – miscellaneous, savoury					
Cobblers[Sa], 2 cobblers	50	180	7	1	Ca
wholemeal, 2 cobblers	50	165	7	3	Ca/Fe/$B_{1,3}$
Dumplings[Sa], 2 dumplings	100	210	12	1	Ca
Pancakes, savoury[Sa], 2 pancakes	70	190	12	1	Ca
made with skimmed milk	70	175	10	1	Ca
Stuffing[Sa], 1 helping	60	140	9	1	A
Yorkshire pudding[Sa], 2 individual	50	105	5	1	Ca
made with skimmed milk	50	95	4	1	Ca
Cheese *Low fat varieties contain 50% less fat*					
Brie[Sa], 1 medium slice	40	120	9	0	Pro/Ca/A/$B_{2,3}$
Camembert[Sa], 1 medium slice	40	120	9	0	Pro/Ca/A/$B_{2,3}$
Cheddar[Sa], 1 medium slice	40	160	13	0	Pro/Ca*/A/$B_{2,3}$
Cheshire[Sa], 1 medium slice	40	160	13	0	Pro/Ca*/A/$B_{2,3}$
Cottage[Sa], 1 helping	45	45	2	0	
Cream, 1 helping	30	130	14	0	A
Strictly not a true cheese					
Danish Blue[Sa], 1 medium slice	40	140	12	0	Pro/Ca/A/$B_{2,3}$
Edam[Sa], 1 medium slice	40	120	9	0	Pro/Ca*/A/$B_{2,3}$
Emmenthal[Sa], 1 medium slice	40	160	13	0	Pro/Ca*/A/$B_{2,3}$
Feta[Sa], 1 medium slice	40	100	8	0	Pro/Ca/A
Gouda[Sa], 1 medium slice	40	120	9	0	Pro/Ca*/A/$B_{2,3}$
Gruyère[Sa], 1 medium slice	40	160	13	0	Pro/Ca*/A/$B_{2,3}$
Parmesan[Sa], 2 heaped tsp	9	35	3	0	Ca
Processed[Sa], 1 slice	20	60	5	0	Ca
Roquefort[Sa], 1 medium slice	40	140	12	0	Pro/Ca/A/$B_{2,3}$

Food, and portion	Wt (g)	En (kcal)	Fat (g)	Fib (g)	Nutrients
St Paulin[Sa], 1 medium slice	40	120	9	0	Pro/Ca*/A/$B_{2,3}$
Stilton[Sa], 1 medium slice	40	185	16	0	Pro/Ca/A/B_3
Cheese dishes and products					
Cauliflower cheese[Sa], 1 helping	310	350	25	4	Pro/Ca*/Fe/A/ $B_{1,2,3}$/C*
Cheese flan[Sa], 1 medium slice	90	280	20	1	Pro/Ca*/Fe/A/B_2,
Cheese omelette[Sa], 2 eggs	195	515	43	0	Pro/Ca*/Fe/A*/D/ $B_{1,2,3}$
Cheese and potato pie[Sa], 1 helping	155	220	12	1	Pro/Ca/A/$B_{2,3}$/C
Cheese pudding[Sa], 1 helping	115	195	12	0	Pro/Ca*/A/$B_{2,3}$
Cheese soufflé[Sa], 1 helping	100	250	19	0	Pro/Ca/Fe/A/D/ $B_{2,3}$
Macaroni cheese[Sa], 1 helping	180	315	19	1	Pro/Ca*/A/$B_{2,3}$
Pizza[Sa], 1 medium slice	160	375	19	3	Pro/Ca*/Fe/A/ $B_{1,2,3}$/C
Quiche Lorraine[Sa], 1 medium slice	90	350	25	1	Pro/Ca/Fe/A/ $B_{1,2,3}$
Welsh rarebit[Sa], 1 slice toast	60	220	14	1	Pro/Ca*/A/B_3
Chocolate					
Bounty[Sa Su], 2 small bars	60	285	16	na	Ca
Chocolate[Su]					
Milk, 1 bar	50	265	15	na	Ca
Plain, 1 bar	50	265	15	na	Fe
Fancy and filled, 1 bar	55	255	10	na	Ca
Mars[Sa Su], 1 bar	65	285	12	na	Ca
Chutney and pickles					
Apple chutney[Sa Su], 1 helping	35	70	0	1	
Piccalilli[Sa Su], 1 helping	40	13	0	1	

Food, and portion	Wt (g)	En (kcal)	Fat (g)	Fib (g)	Nutrients
Sweet pickle[Sa Su], 1 helping *e.g. Branston, Pan Yan*	35	45	0	1	
Tomato chutney[Sa Su], 1 helping	35	55	0	1	
Cream					
With drinks and soups					
double, 1 helping	25	110	12	0	A
single, 1 helping	25	55	5	0	
whipping, 1 helping	25	85	9	0	A
With puddings – on a medium portion of a pudding					
double, 1 helping	35	155	17	0	A
single, 1 helping	35	75	7	0	A
whipping, 1 helping	35	115	12	0	A
Aerosol cream may contain added sugar					
Crumpets, muffins and scones					
Crumpets[Sa], toasted, 2 crumpets	60	120	1	2	Ca/B_1
Muffins[Sa Su]					
bran, 1 muffin	70	190	5	6	Ca/Fe/$B_{1,3}$
plain, 1 muffin	70	200	4	2	Pro/Ca/Fe/$B_{1,3}$
Scones					
cheese[Sa], 1 scone	50	180	9	1	Ca/A
fruit[Sa Su], 1 scone	50	160	5	2	Ca/B_1
plain[Sa Su], 1 scone	50	180	7	1	Ca
wholemeal[Sa Su], 1 scone	50	165	7	3	Ca/Fe/$B_{1,3}$
wholemeal fruit[Sa Su], 1 scone	50	160	6	3	Ca/Fe/$B_{1,3}$
Eggs					
Boiled egg, 1 size 2	60	90	7	0	Pro/Fe/A/D/$B_{2,3}$
Fried egg, 1 size 2	60	140	12	0	Pro/Fe/A/D/$B_{2,3}$
Poached egg, 1 size 2	60	95	7	0	Pro/Fe/A/D/$B_{2,3}$

Food, and portion	Wt (g)	En (kcal)	Fat (g)	Fib (g)	Nutrients
Egg dishes and products					
Egg and bacon pie[Sa], 1 medium slice	155	465	30	2	Pro/Ca/Fe/A/D/$B_{1, 2, 3}$
Omelette[Sa], 2 eggs	135	255	22	0	Pro/Ca/Fe/A/D/$B_{2, 3}$
Scotch egg[Sa], 1 egg	120	335	25	0	Pro/Ca/Fe/$B_{2, 3}$
Scrambled egg[Sa], 2 eggs	140	345	32	0	Pro/Ca/Fe/A/D/$B_{2, 3}$
Fat *Unsalted butter and low-fat spread are available*					
Fat spread on bread from a large loaf and both sides of a bread roll					
butter[Sa], medium spread	8	60	6	0	A
low-fat spread[Sa], medium spread	8	30	3	0	
margarine[Sa], medium spread	8	60	6	0	
Fat spread on crackers, crispbread and water biscuits					
butter[Sa], medium spread	3	20	2	0	
low-fat spread[Sa], medium spread	3	11	1	0	
margarine[Sa], medium spread	3	20	2	0	
Fat served with a medium size jacket potato					
butter[Sa], medium chunk	10	75	8	0	A
low-fat spread[Sa], medium chunk	10	35	4	0	A
margarine[Sa], medium chunk	10	75	8	0	A
Fish					
Cod steak, grilled, 2 steaks	130	125	2	0	Pro/$B_{1, 3}$
Cod in batter, fried[Sa], 1 piece *Some brands have added sugar in the coating*	85	170	9	0	Pro/Ca/B_3
Crab white meat, canned[Sa Su], 1 helping	70	55	1	0	Pro/Ca/Fe/B_3

Food, and portion	Wt (g)	En (kcal)	Fat (g)	Fib (g)	Nutrients
Herring fillets in oatmeal, fried, 2 fillets	110	255	17	2	Pro/Fe/D*/$B_{2,3}$*
Kipper fillets, baked[Sa], 2 fillets	130	265	15	0	Pro*/Ca/Fe/D*/$B_{2,3}$*
Mackerel fillets, fried, 2 fillets	110	205	12	0	Pro/Fe/D*/$B_{2,3}$*
Pilchards in tomato sauce, canned[Sa], 1 helping	105	130	6	0	Pro/Ca*/Fe/D*/$B_{2,3}$*
Plaice fillets, steamed, 2 small fillets	120	110	2	0	Pro/$B_{1,3}$
Plaice fillets in crumbs, fried, 1 fillet	105	240	14	0	Pro/Ca/$B_{1,2,3}$
Prawns, peeled[Sa], 1 helping	80	85	1	0	Pro/Ca/B_3
Rock salmon in batter fried[Sa], chip shop	205	545	39	1	Pro*/Ca/Fe/$B_{1,2,3}$*
Salmon cutlets, steamed, 1 cutlet	135	215	14	0	Pro/$B_{1,3}$*
Salmon red, canned, skin and bone removed, 1 helping	115	180	9	0	Pro/Ca/Fe/A/D*/$B_{2,3}$*
Salmon, smoked[Sa], 1 helping	60	85	3	0	Pro/B_3
Sardines in oil, canned[Sa] oil drained off, 1 helping	70	150	10	0	Pro/Ca*/Fe/D*/$B_{2,3}$
Sardines in tomato sauce, canned[Sa], 1 helping	85	150	10	0	Pro/Ca*/Fe/D*, $B_{2,3}$
Scampi fried[Sa], 9 pieces	80	255	14	1	Pro/Ca/B_3
Some brands have added sugar in the coating					
Tuna in oil canned[Sa] oil drained off, 1 helping	95	275	21	0	Pro/Fe/D*/B_3*
Fish dishes and products					
Cod roe in crumbs, fried[Sa], chip shop	80	160	10	0	Pro/Fe/A/D/$B_{1,2,3}$*/C*
Fish cakes, fried[Sa], 2 fish cakes	110	205	12	1	Pro/Ca/Fe/B_3

Food, and portion	Wt (g)	En (kcal)	Fat (g)	Fib (g)	Nutrients
Fish curry[Sa]					
haddock, 1 helping	175	445	39	na	Pro/Ca/Fe/Å/ $B_{1,3}$/C
herring, 1 helping	175	610	57	na	Pro/Ca/Fe/Å/Ḋ/ $B_{2,3}$/C
Fish fingers, fried[Sa], 4 fish fingers	100	235	13	1	Pro/B_2
Some brands have added sugar in the coating					
Fish pie[Sa], 1 helping	265	340	15	2	Pro/Ca/Fe/A/ $B_{1,2,3}$/C
Kedgeree[Sa], 1 helping	160	240	11	0	Pro/Ca/Fe/A/D/ $B_{1,2,3}$
Taramasalata[Sa], 1 helping	100	445	46	na	
Fruit, canned in syrup *Fruit canned without added sugar is available*					
Apricots[Su], 5 halves	140	150	0	2	A
Fruit salad[Su], 1 helping	130	125	0	1	Fe/C
Grapefruit[Su], 6 segments	120	70	0	0	Ċ
Guavas[Su], 6 halves	175	105	0	6	Ċ
Lychees[Su], 10 lychees	150	100	0	1	Fe/C
Mandarin oranges[Su], 16 segments	115	65	0	0	Ċ
Mango[Su], 2 slices	135	105	0	1	A/C
Peaches[Su], 6 slices	110	95	0	1	C
Pears[Su], 3 quarters	135	105	0	2	
Pineapple[Su], 11 cubes	150	115	0	1	Ċ
Raspberries[Su], 15 raspberries	90	80	0	5	Fe/C
Strawberries[Su], 10 strawberries	85	70	0	1	Ċ
Fruit, dried					
Apricots, 8	50	90	0	12	Fe/A/B_3
Currants, 2 handfuls	35	85	0	2	

Food, and portion	Wt (g)	En (kcal)	Fat (g)	Fib (g)	Nutrients
Dates, 9	40	100	0	3	
Dates may be coated with sugar					
Figs, 4	60	130	0	11	Ca/Fe
Prunes, 8	40	55	0	5	
weighed with stones					
Raisins, 2 handfuls	35	85	0	2	
Sultanas, 2 handfuls	35	90	0	2	
Fruit, fresh					
Apples, eating, 1 medium	120	40	0	2	
weighed with skin and core					
Apricots, 3	110	30	0	2	A/C
weighed with stones					
Avocado pear, ½ medium pear	90	200	20	2	Fe/C
weight of flesh only					
Bananas, 1 medium	135	65	0	3	C
weighed with skin					
Blackberries, 15	80	25	0	6	Ca/C*
Cherries, 12	100	40	0	2	C
weighed with stones					
Figs, green, 1	85	35	0	2	
stalks removed					
Gooseberries, ripe, 11	70	25	0	2	C*
topped and tailed					
Grapes black, medium bunch	140	70	0	0	C
white, medium bunch	140	85	0	1	C
Grapefruit, ½ medium	140	15	0	0	C*
weighed with peel and pips					
Lemon, 1 wedge	25	4	0	1	C*
Mango, 1 medium	185	110	0	3	A/C*
weight of flesh only					

Food, and portion	Wt (g)	En (kcal)	Fat (g)	Fib (g)	Nutrients
Melons					
weighed with skin					
Canteloupe, ½ melon	360	55	0	2	Fe/Å/B₁/Č
Honeydew, 1 medium slice	190	25	0	1	Č
Water, 1 medium slice	320	35	0	na	C
Nectarine, 1 medium	110	50	0	2	A/C
weighed with stone					
Orange, 1 medium	245	65	0	4	Ca/B₁/Č
weighed with peel and pips					
Passion fruit, 4	170	25	0	11	C
weighed with skin					
Peach, 1 medium	125	40	0	2	A/C
weighed with stone					
Pear, eating, 1 medium	150	45	0	3	C
weighed with skin and core					
Pineapple, 1 medium slice	125	60	0	2	B₁/Č
weight of flesh only					
Plums, dessert, 3	105	40	0	2	C
weighed with stones					
Raspberries, 15	70	18	0	5	Č
Strawberries, 1 helping	100	25	0	2	Č
stalks removed					
Tangerine, 1 medium	100	25	0	1	Č
weighed with peel and pips					
Meat					
Bacon joints[Sa]					
collar boiled					
meat and fat, 1 helping	55	180	15	0	Pro/$B_{1,3}$
meat only, 1 helping	55	105	5	0	Pro/Fe/$B_{1,2,3}$
gammon boiled					
meat and fat, 1 helping	55	150	10	0	Pro/$B_{1,3}$

Food, and portion	Wt (g)	En (kcal)	Fat (g)	Fib (g)	Nutrients
meat only, 1 helping	55	90	3	0	$\underline{\text{Pro}}/B_{1, 3}$
Bacon rashers[Sa]					
back grilled					
meat and fat, 3 rashers	45	180	15	0	$\underline{\text{Pro}}/B_{1, 3}$
meat only, 4 rashers	45	130	9	0	$\underline{\text{Pro}}/B_{1, 3}$
served trimmed of visible fat					
streaky grilled					
meat and fat, 4 rashers	40	170	14	0	$\underline{\text{Pro}}/B_{1, 3}$
Bacon steaks[Sa]					
gammon grilled					
meat and fat, 1 steak	120	275	15	0	$\underline{\text{Pro}}^*/\text{Fe}/B^*_{1, 2, 3^*}$
meat only, 1 steak	120	205	6	0	$\underline{\text{Pro}}^*/\text{Fe}/B^*_{1, 2, 3^*}$
purchased without visible fat					
Sweetcure bacon contains added sugar					
Beef joints					
silverside boiled					
meat and fat, 1 helping	55	135	8	0	$\underline{\text{Pro}}/\text{Fe}/B_{3}$
meat only, 1 helping	55	95	3	0	$\underline{\text{Pro}}/\text{Fe}/B_{2, 3}$
topside roast					
meat and fat, 1 helping	55	120	7	0	$\underline{\text{Pro}}/\text{Fe}/B_{2, 3}$
meat only, 1 helping	55	85	2	0	$\underline{\text{Pro}}/\text{Fe}/B_{2, 3}$
Beef steaks					
rump grilled					
meat and fat, 1 steak	155	340	19	0	$\underline{\text{Pro}}^*/\text{Fe}^*/B_{1, 2, 3^*}$
meat only, 1 steak	155	260	9	0	$\underline{\text{Pro}}^*/\text{Fe}^*/B_{1, 2, 3^*}$
purchased without visible fat					
Lamb chops served whole					
loin chops grilled					
meat and fat, 2 chops	160	445	36	0	$\underline{\text{Pro}}/\text{Fe}/B_{1, 2, 3^*}$
meat only, 2 chops	160	195	11	0	$\underline{\text{Pro}}/\text{Fe}/B_{1, 2, 3^*}$

Food, and portion	Wt (g)	En (kcal)	Fat (g)	Fib (g)	Nutrients
Lamb joints					
breast roast					
meat and fat, 1 helping	55	225	20	0	Pro/B_3
meat only, 1 helping	55	140	9	0	Pro/B_3
leg roast					
meat and fat, 1 helping	55	145	10	0	Pro/Fe/$B_{2,3}$
meat only, 1 helping	55	105	4	0	Pro/Fe/$B_{2,3}$
Pork chops served whole					
loin grilled					
meat and fat, 1 chop	135	350	25	0	Pro/Fe/$B^{*}_{1,2,3^{*}}$
meat only, 1 chop	135	180	9	0	Pro/Fe/$B^{*}_{1,2,3^{*}}$
Pork joints					
leg roast					
meat and fat, 1 helping	55	155	11	0	Pro/$B_{1,3}$
meat only, 1 helping	55	100	4	0	Pro/$B_{1,2,3}$
Pork rashers					
belly grilled					
meat and fat, 2 rashers	200	795	70	0	Pro*/Fe/$B^{*}_{1,2,3^{*}}$
Meat, canned					
Chopped ham and pork[Sa], 2 medium slices	60	160	14	0	Pro/$B_{1,3}$
Corned beef[Sa], 2 medium slices	60	130	7	0	Pro/Fe/B_3
Ham[Sa Su], 2 medium slices	55	65	3	0	Pro/$B_{1,3}$
Luncheon meat[Sa Su], 2 medium slices	70	220	19	0	Pro/B_3
Meat dishes and products					
Beefburgers fried[Sa], 2 burgers *some brands have added sugar*	90	240	16	0	Pro/Fe/$B_{2,3}$
Beef kheema, 1 helping	190	780	71	0	Pro*/Fe*/A/$B_{2,3^{*}}$
Beef koftas[Sa], 5 koftas	80	280	22	0	Pro/Fe/B_3

Food, and portion	Wt (g)	En (kcal)	Fat (g)	Fib (g)	Nutrients
Beef stew[Sa], 1 helping	175	210	13	1	Pro/Fe/Å/$B_{2, 3}$
Bolognese sauce[Sa], 1 helping	140	195	15	0	Pro/Fe/Å/$B_{2, 3}$/C
Chilli-con-carne[Sa], 1 helping	235	350	20	8	Pro/Ca/Fe*/A/ $B_{1, 2, \overset{*}{3}}$/C
Cornish pasty[Sa], 1 pasty	255	845	52	3	Pro/Ca/Fe/$B_{1, 3}$
Hotpot[Sa], 1 helping	195	220	8	3	Pro/Fe/Å/$B_{1, 2, 3}$/ C
Irish stew, 1 helping meat on the bone	255	290	17	3	Pro/Fe/$B_{1, 3}$/C
Kebab, Indian[Sa], 1 kebab	155	555	40	na	Pro*/Ca/Fe*/A/D/ $B_{1, 2, \overset{*}{3}}$/C
Lasagne[Sa], 1 helping	230	345	20	1	Pro/Ca/Fe/A/$B_{2, 3}$
Meat and vegetable pie, shortcrust pastry top and bottom, 1 medium slice	130	450	28	2	Pro/Ca/Fe/A/$B_{1, 3}$
Meat loaf[Sa], 1 medium slice	100	280	19	1	Pro/Fe/$B_{2, 3}$
Mince stewed with onion[Sa], 1 helping	165	315	24	1	Pro/Fe/B_3
Lean mince stewed with onion, 1 helping	165	215	11	1	Pro/Fe/$B_{2, 3}$
Mince stewed with vegetables[Sa], 1 helping	170	250	18	1	Pro/Fe/Å/B_3
Lean mince stewed with vegetables, 1 helping	170	185	9	1	Pro/Fe/Å/$B_{2, 3}$
Moussaka[Sa], 1 helping	160	310	21	1	Pro/Ca/Fe/$B_{2, 3}$/C
Mutton biriani[Sa], 1 helping	225	560	31	na	Pro/Ca/Fe/A/ $B_{1, 2, 3}$/C
Pork pie[Sa Su], 1 individual	150	565	41	2	Pro/Ca/Fe/$B_{1, 3}$
Ravioli in tomato sauce, canned[Sa Su], 1 helping	145	100	3	1	Fe/B_3

Food, and portion	Wt (g)	En (kcal)	Fat (g)	Fib (g)	Nutrients
Samosa, meat, 2 samosas	110	650	62	2	B_3
Shepherd's pie[Sa], 1 helping	165	195	10	1	Pro/Fe/$B_{2,3}$/C
Steak and kidney pie[Sa],					
flaky pastry top, 1 medium slice	140	400	26	1	Pro/Ca/Fe/A/ $B_{1,2,3}^{*}$
flaky pastry top and bottom, 1 individual	165	535	35	2	Pro/Ca/Fe/$B_{1,2,3}$
Note: Unfortified fat used in shop-bought pie therefore no vitamin A					
Steak and kidney pudding[Sa], 1 medium slice	160	355	19	1	Pro/Ca/Fe/$B_{1,2,}$

Milk

Food, and portion	Wt (g)	En (kcal)	Fat (g)	Fib (g)	Nutrients
For drinking or as part of a 'milky' drink – average of glass, cup and mug					
milk, approx ⅓pt	195	125	7	0	Pro/Ca/A/B_2
semi-skimmed, approx ⅓pt	195	95	4	0	Pro/Ca/B_2/C
skimmed, approx ⅓pt	195	65	0	0	Pro/Ca*/B_2/C
In tea or coffee – average of cup and mug					
milk, medium serving	35	25	1	0	
semi-skimmed, medium serving	35	15	1	0	
skimmed, medium serving	35	12	0	0	
With breakfast cereals – on a medium portion of cereal					
milk, medium serving	115	75	4	0	Ca/B_2
semi-skimmed, medium serving	115	55	2	0	Ca/B_2
skimmed, medium serving	115	40	0	0	Ca/B_2
With puddings – on a medium portion of a pudding					
Condensed milk whole[Su], medium serving sweetened	45	145	4	0	Ca/B_2
Evaporated milk whole, medium serving unsweetened	30	45	3	0	Ca

Food, and portion	Wt (g)	En (kcal)	Fat (g)	Fib (g)	Nutrients
Nuts and seeds For nuts the weight given is for kernels only and medium-size portions					
Almonds, 20	20	115	11	3	Ca/B_2
Brazil nuts, 9	30	185	18	3	Ca/B_1
Cashew nuts, 20	40	225	18	na	Pro/Fe/B_1
Hazelnuts, 30	25	95	9	2	B_1
Peanuts, 32	30	170	15	2	Pro/$B_{1, 3}$
Strictly peanuts are pulses and not nuts					
Sesame seeds, sprinkling	15	90	8	na	Fe/$B_{1, 3}$
Walnuts, 9 halves	25	130	13	1	
Offal					
Kidney lamb's, fried, 1 helping	75	115	5	0	Pro/Fe*/A/$B_{1, 2*, 3*}$/C
Liver lamb's, fried, 1 helping	90	210	13	0	Pro/Fe*/A*/$B_{1, 2*, 3*}$/C
Offal dishes and products					
Faggots[Sa], 2 faggots	190	510	35	1	Pro/Ca/Fe*/A*/$B_{1, 2*, 3*}$
Heart casserole[Sa], 1 helping	160	150	7	2	Pro/Fe/A*/$B_{1, 2, 3}$
Liver sausage[Sa], 4 slices	35	110	9	0	Fe/A*/$B_{2, 3}$
Liver and onion stew[Sa], 1 helping	125	210	14	1	Pro/Fe*/A*/$B_{1, 2*, 3*}$
Pâté[Sa], 1 helping	60	185	16	0	Pro/Fe/A*/$B_{1, 2*, 3}$
Some brands have added sugar					
Tongue, canned[Sa], 2 medium slices	50	105	8	0	Pro/Fe/$B_{2, 3}$
Tripe and onions[Sa], 1 helping	165	135	5	1	Pro/Ca/B_3
Pasta					
Spaghetti[Sa]					
white, boiled, 1 helping	150	155	1	3	B_3

Food, and portion	Wt (g)	En (kcal)	Fat (g)	Fib (g)	Nutrients
wholemeal, boiled, 1 helping	150	170	1	6	Pro/Fe/$B_{1,3}$
Pasta products *Wholemeal varieties contain more than double the amount of fibre*					
Spaghetti canned					
in Bolognese sauce[Sa Su], 1 helping	125	110	4	2	B_3
in tomato sauce[Sa Su], 1 helping	125	80	1	4	
Poultry					
Chicken roast					
meat and skin, 1 helping	55	120	8	0	Pro/B_3
meat only, 1 helping	55	80	3	0	Pro/B_3
leg quarter, 1 leg quarter	190	175	6	0	Pro/$B_{2,3}$*
wing quarter, 1 wing quarter	230	170	6	0	Pro/$B_{2,3}$*
Duck roast					
meat and skin, 1 helping	55	185	16	0	Pro/Fe/B_3
meat only, 1 helping	55	105	5	0	Pro/Fe/$B_{1,2,3}$
Turkey roast					
meat and skin, 1 helping	55	95	4	0	Pro/B_3
meat only, 1 helping	55	75	1	0	Pro/B_3
Poultry dishes					
Chicken casserole[Sa], 1 helping	195	185	10	1	Pro/Fe/A*/$B_{1,3}$
Chicken curry[Sa], 1 helping	245	580	51	1	Pro/Ca/Fe/A*/B
Chicken pie[Sa]					
shortcrust pastry top and bottom, 1 medium slice	140	475	28	2	Pro/Ca/Fe/A/D/ $B_{1,3}$
flaky pastry top, 1 medium slice	160	470	31	1	Pro/Ca/Fe/A/D/ $B_{1,2,3}$*
Chicken in white sauce[Sa], 1 helping	155	230	12	0	Pro/Ca/$B_{1,2,3}$*

Food, and portion	Wt (g)	En (kcal)	Fat (g)	Fib (g)	Nutrients
Puddings					
Bakewell tart[Sa Su], 1 medium slice	90	410	27	2	Ca/Fe/A/D/B_3
Bread and butter pudding[Sa Su], 1 helping	130	210	10	0	Pro/Ca/A/$B_{2,3}$
Bread pudding[Sa Su], 1 helping	190	565	18	6	Pro/Ca/Fe/A/$B_{1,2,3}$
Custard tart[Sa Su], 1 medium slice	85	240	14	1	Ca/A
Eve's pudding[Sa Su], 1 helping	105	255	14	2	Ca/A/D/C
Fruit					
Apple					
baked with sugar[Su], 1 medium apple	125	95	0	3	C
Without added sugar gives about 50% less energy					
stewed with sugar[Su], 1 helping	120	80	0	2	C
without sugar, 1 helping	120	40	0	3	C
Fruit crumble[Sa Su], 1 helping	120	240	8	3	Ca/A/C
wholemeal, 1 helping	120	230	9	4	Fe/A/B_3/C
Fruit flan					
pastry[Sa Su], 1 medium slice	80	95	4	1	C
sponge[Su], 1 medium slice	60	65	1	0	C
Fruit pie[Sa Su], 1 medium slice	120	225	9	3	Ca/C
wholemeal, 1 medium slice	120	220	10	4	Fe/B_3/C
Fruit salad, fresh, 1 helping	185	100	0	4	C*
Gulab jamen[Su], 1 helping	75	270	11	0	Ca/A/D/B_2
Ice cream[Su]					
Arctic roll, 1 medium slice	30	60	2	0	
dairy ice cream, 1 helping	75	125	5	na	Ca
non-dairy ice cream, 1 helping	75	125	6	na	Ca
Instant desserts[Sa Su], 1 sundae glass	90	100	6	0	Ca

Food, and portion	Wt (g)	En (kcal)	Fat (g)	Fib (g)	Nutrients
made with skimmed milk, 1 sundae glass	90	75	3	0	Ca
Jellabi[Su], 1 helping	50	180	7	1	
Jelly[Su], 1 helping	135	80	0	na	
made with milk, 1 helping	135	115	2	na	Ca
Lemon meringue pie[Sa Su], 1 medium slice	95	305	14	1	A
Pancakes, sweet[Su], 2 pancakes	70	210	11	1	Ca
made with skimmed milk	70	195	10	1	Ca
Queen of puddings[Sa Su], 1 helping	125	265	10	1	Ca/A/B_2
Rice pudding[Su], 1 helping	85	110	4	0	Ca
made with skimmed milk, 1 helping	85	80	0	0	Ca
Sevyiaan[Sa Su], 1 helping	125	555	35	3	Ca/Fe/A/B_3
Sponge pudding[Sa Su]					
with dried fruit, 1 helping	95	315	14	2	Ca/Fe/A/D
with jam or treacle, 1 helping	95	315	14	1	Ca/Fe/A/D
Treacle tart[Sa Su], 1 medium slice	70	260	10	1	
Trifle[Su]					
with Dream Topping, 1 helping	175	260	8	1	Pro/Ca/A/$B_{1, 2}$/C
with fresh cream, 1 helping	175	290	16	1	Ca/A/$B_{1, 2}$/C

Pulse dishes and products

Food, and portion	Wt (g)	En (kcal)	Fat (g)	Fib (g)	Nutrients
Baked beans in tomato sauce, canned[Sa Su], 1 helping	200	130	1	15	Pro/Ca/Fe/$B_{1, 3}$
Some brands do not have added sugar					
Dahl[Sa]					
chick pea, 1 helping	155	225	5	9	Pro/Ca/Fe/A/$B_{1, 3}$/C

Food, and portion	Wt (g)	En (kcal)	Fat (g)	Fib (g)	Nutrients
lentil, 1 helping	155	140	5	4	Pro/Fe/B_1
Hummus[Sa], 1 helping	65	120	8	na	Fe/B_1
Pea curry[Sa], 1 helping	125	440	42	5	Fe/Å/$B_{1,3}$/C
Pea and potato curry[Sa], 1 helping	200	285	22	6	Ca/Fe/A/$B_{1,3}$/C
Soya milk, 1 glass	200	80	na	na	
Some brands have added salt and sugar					
Tofu steamed, 1 helping	60	40	3	0	Ca*
Rice					
Brown, boiled[Sa], 1 helping	165	235	2	2	$B_{1,3}$
White, boiled[Sa], 1 helping	165	205	0	1	
Rice dishes					
Fried, rice[Sa], 1 helping	190	250	6	2	
Pilau rice[Sa], 1 helping	190	410	22	3	Fe/$B_{1,3}$
Risotto, plain[Sa], 1 helping	315	705	29	4	Pro/Ca/A/D/$B_{1,3}$
As the basis of a meal and not as an accompaniment					
Savoury rice[Sa], 1 helping	190	270	7	2	$B_{1,3}$
Salad/raw vegetables					
Beansprouts, 1 helping	85	30	0	na	Fe/B_1/Č
Beetroot					
grated, 1 helping	35	10	0	1	
boiled sliced, 1 helping	40	18	0	1	
Brussels sprouts grated, 1 helping	55	14	0	2	Č
Cabbage					
red, shredded, 1 helping	55	11	0	2	Č
white, shredded, 1 helping	55	12	0	1	Č
Carrot, grated, 1 helping	35	8	0	1	Å
Cauliflower florets, 1 helping	50	7	0	1	Č
Celery sticks, 1 helping	40	3	0	1	
Chicory, 1 helping	45	4	0	na	

Food, and portion	Wt (g)	En (kcal)	Fat (g)	Fib (g)	Nutrients
Cucumber sliced, 1 helping	30	3	0	0	
Endive, 1 helping	40	4	0	1	Fe/A/C
Lettuce, 1 helping	30	4	0	0	C
Mushrooms sliced, 1 helping	35	5	0	1	
Mustard and cress, 1 helping	15	2	0	1	C
Onion, rings, 1 helping	30	7	0	0	C
spring, 3 medium	15	5	0	0	C
Parsley chopped, sprinkling	4	1	0	0	C
Peppers sweet, sliced, 1 helping	45	7	0	0	C*
Radishes, 4 medium	50	8	0	1	C
Tomatoes, 2 medium	150	20	0	2	A/C*
Watercress, 1 helping	15	2	0	0	A/C

Sauces – savoury *Sauces may be low calorie and without added salt and sugar*

Food, and portion	Wt (g)	En (kcal)	Fat (g)	Fib (g)	Nutrients
Apple purée, 1 helping	80	25	0	2	C
Bread sauce[Sa], 1 helping	80	90	4	0	Ca
Brown sauce, bottled[Sa Su], 1 helping	9	9	0	na	
Cheese sauce[Sa], 1 helping	80	160	12	0	Pro/Ca/A/B_2
French dressing[Sa Su], 1 helping	9	60	7	0	
Gravy[Sa]					
cornflour based, 1 helping	80	20	1	na	
meat juice based, 1 helping	80	85	8	na	
Mayonnaise[Sa Su], 1 helping	20	145	16	na	
Onion sauce[Sa], 1 helping	80	80	5	1	Ca
Salad cream[Sa Su], 1 helping	15	45	4	na	
Tomato ketchup[Sa Su], 1 helping	20	20	0	na	
Tomato sauce[Sa], 1 helping	80	70	4	2	A/C
White sauce[Sa], 1 helping	80	120	8	0	Ca/A

Food, and portion	Wt (g)	En (kcal)	Fat (g)	Fib (g)	Nutrients
Sauces – sweet With puddings – on a medium portion of a pudding					
Custard[Sa Su], 1 helping	75	90	3	0	Ca
made with skimmed milk, 1 helping	75	60	0	0	Ca
Dream Topping[Su], 1 helping	35	65	5	0	
made with skimmed milk, 1 helping	35	55	4	0	
Egg custard sauce[Su], 1 helping	75	90	5	0	Ca/B_2
White sauce[Su], 1 helping	75	130	7	0	Ca
Sausages					
Frankfurters[Sa Su], 3	90	245	23	0	Pro/Fe/B_3
Salami[Sa], 5 slices	55	270	25	0	Pro/$B_{1,3}$
Sausages[Sa]					
beef grilled, 2	90	240	16	1	Pro/Ca/Fe/B_3
pork grilled, 2	90	285	22	0	Pro/Fe/B_3
Fried sausages contain more fat than grilled sausages because during grilling fat drains away. Low-fat sausages contain half the fat of full-fat sausages.					
Saveloy[Sa], 1	75	195	15	0	Pro/Fe/$B_{1,3}$
Sausage dishes and products					
Sausage rolls[Sa], 1 sausage roll	65	310	24	1	A/B_3
Toad in the hole[Sa], 1 helping	135	385	28	1	Pro/Ca/Fe/$B_{2,3}$
Savoury snacks and nibbles					
Chevda[Sa], 1 packet	100	495	32	6	Pro/Ca/Fe*/A/$B_{1,3^*}$
Cashew nuts roasted and salted[Sa], 1 small packet	25	140	11	na	B_1
Crisps[Sa], 1 packet	30	160	11	4	B_3/C
Low-fat crisps contain about 30% less fat					
Gherkins[Sa], 7 mini	20	3	na	0	

Food, and portion	Wt (g)	En (kcal)	Fat (g)	Fib (g)	Nutrients
Olives black with stones^{Sa}, 9	35	30	3	1	
Peanuts roasted and salted^{Sa}, 1 small packet	25	145	12	2	B_3
Some types of salted peanuts also contain added sugar					
Pistachio nuts roasted and salted^{Sa}, 1 packet	50	165	14	na	Fe/B_1
Soft drinks and fruit juices *Low-calorie and sugar-free soft drinks are available*					
Coca-cola^{Su}, 1 glass	200	80	0	0	
Grapefruit juice, canned					
sweetened^{Su}, 1 glass	200	75	0	0	C*
unsweetened, 1 glass	200	60	0	0	C*
Lemon juice, fresh, 2 tsp	10	1	0	0	C
Lemonade^{Su}, 1 glass	200	40	0	0	
Lime cordial, undiluted^{Su}, for 1 glass	45	50	0	0	
Lucozade^{Su}, 1 glass	200	135	0	0	C
Orange juice					
fresh, 1 small glass	70	25	0	0	C*
canned sweetened^{Su}, 1 glass	200	100	0	0	B_1/C*
canned unsweetened, 1 glass	200	65	0	0	Fe/B_1C*
Orange squash, undiluted^{Su}, for 1 glass	45	50	0	0	
Pineapple juice, canned^{Su}, 1 glass	200	105	0	0	Fe/B_1/C*
Ribena, undiluted^{Su}, for, 1 glass	45	105	0	0	C*
Tomato juice, canned, 1 glass	200	30	0	0	Fe/A/B_1/C*
Soups, canned					
Chicken, cream of$^{Sa\ Su}$, 1 helping	145	85	6	na	
Mushroom, cream of$^{Sa\ Su}$, 1 helping	145	75	6	na	

Food, and portion	Wt (g)	En (kcal)	Fat (g)	Fib (g)	Nutrients
Oxtail[Sa Su], 1 helping	145	65	2	na	Ca/Fe
Tomato, cream of[Sa Su], 1 helping	145	80	5	na	
Vegetable[Sa Su], 1 helping	145	55	1	na	
Spreads – savoury Spread on bread from a large loaf					
Bovril[Sa], medium spread	4	7	0	0	$B_{1, 2, 3}$
Cheese spread[Sa], 1 triangle	15	40	3	0	Ca
Fish paste[Sa], medium spread	9	15	1	0	
Marmite[Sa], medium spread	4	7	0	0	$B_{1, 2, 3}$
Meat paste[Sa], medium spread	9	16	1	0	
Peanut butter[Sa Su], medium spread	7	45	4	1	
Some brands of peanut butter do not contain added sugar					
Spreads – sweet Spread on bread from a large loaf					
Honey[Su], medium spread	10	30	0	0	
Jam with seeds[Su], medium spread *e.g. blackberry, blackcurrant, gooseberry, raspberry, strawberry*	10	25	0	0	
Jam from stone fruit[Su], medium spread *e.g. apricot, damson, greengage, plum*	10	25	0	0	
Fruit spreads without added sugar and low-sugar jams are available					
Lemon curd[Su]					
egg based, medium spread	10	30	1	0	
starch based, medium spread	10	30	1	0	
Marmalade[Su], medium spread	10	25	0	0	
Sugar					
Honey, 1 level tsp	7	20	0	na	
Sugar					
brown, 1 level tsp	5	20	0	0	
white, 1 level tsp	5	20	0	0	

Food, and portion	Wt (g)	En (kcal)	Fat (g)	Fib (g)	Nutrients
Sweets					
Boiled sweets[Su], approx ¼lb	100	325	0	0	
Fruit gums[Su], 1 packet	30	50	0	na	Ca/Fe
Fruit pastilles[Su], 1 packet	40	100	0	na	
Liquorice allsorts[Sa Su], approx ¼lb	100	315	2	na	Ca/Fe*
Peppermints[Su], 1 packet	30	120	0	0	
Popcorn candied[Sa Su], 1 packet	100	480	20	na	A
Toffees[Sa Su], approx ¼lb	100	430	17	na	Ca/Fe
Vegetables cooked					
Artichokes					
globe boiled[Sa], 1 medium	220	15	0	na	C
Jerusalem boiled[Sa], 1 helping	120	20	0	na	
Asparagus boiled[Sa], 4 spears	120	11	0	1	C
Beans					
broad, boiled[Sa], 1 helping	75	35	0	3	B_3/C
butter, boiled[Sa], 1 helping	75	70	0	4	Fe
French, boiled[Sa], 1 helping	105	7	0	3	C
haricot, boiled[Sa], 1 helping	105	100	1	8	<u>Pro</u>/Ca/Fe
red kidney, boiled[Sa], 1 helping	105	100	1	8	<u>Pro</u>/Ca/Fe
runner, boiled[Sa], 1 helping	105	20	0	4	C
Beansprouts, canned[Sa], 1 helping	80	7	0	2	
Broccoli, boiled[Sa], 1 helping	95	17	0	4	Ca/A*/B_2/C*
Brussels sprouts, boiled[Sa], 1 helping	115	20	0	3	A/C*
Cabbage, boiled[Sa], 1 helping	75	7	0	2	C
Carrots, boiled[Sa], 1 helping	65	12	0	2	A*
Cauliflower, boiled[Sa], 1 helping	100	9	0	2	C*
Celery, boiled[Sa], 1 helping	60	3	0	1	C
Corn canned kernels[Sa Su], 1 helping	70	55	0	4	C

Food, and portion	Wt (g)	En (kcal)	Fat (g)	Fib (g)	Nutrients
Leeks, boiled[Sa], 1 helping	125	30	0	5	Ca/Fe/$\overset{*}{C}$
Marrow, boiled[Sa], 1 helping	90	6	0	1	
Mixed vegetables, boiled[Sa], 1 helping	75	30	0	3	$\overset{*}{A}$/C
Mushrooms, fried, 1 helping	55	115	12	2	$B_{2,3}$
Onions, fried, 1 helping	40	140	13	2	
Parsnips, boiled[Sa], 1 helping	110	60	0	3	C
Peas					
frozen, boiled[Sa], 1 helping	75	30	0	9	Fe/$B_{1,3}$/C
garden, canned[Sa Su], 1 helping	85	40	0	5	Fe/$B_{1,3}$/C
marrowfat, processed[Sa Su], 1 helping	85	70	0	7	Fe
Plantain					
green, boiled[Sa], 1 helping	85	105	0	5	
ripe, fried, 1 helping	80	215	7	5	C
Potatoes					
boiled[Sa], 1 helping	150	120	0	2	B_1/C
chips, chip shop	265	670	29	na	<u>Pro</u>/Fe/$B_{1,3}$/$\overset{*}{C}$
Lower fat chips may contain about 30% less fat					
jacket, 1 medium potato	140	145	0	4	Fe/$B_{1,3}$/C
mashed[Sa], 1 helping	170	200	9	2	$B_{1,3}$/C
roast[Sa], 1 helping	130	205	6	na	$B_{1,3}$/C
sweet, boiled[Sa], 1 helping	150	130	1	3	$\overset{*}{A}$/B_1/$\overset{*}{C}$
Spinach, boiled[Sa], 1 helping	130	40	1	8	<u>Pro</u>/$\overset{*}{Ca}$/$\overset{*}{Fe}$/$\overset{*}{A}$/ $B_{2,3}$/$\overset{*}{C}$
Spring greens, boiled[Sa], 1 helping	75	8	0	3	Ca/$\overset{*}{A}$/$\overset{*}{C}$
Swede, boiled[Sa], 1 helping	120	20	0	3	Ca/$\overset{*}{C}$
Tomatoes					
canned, 1 helping	140	17	0	1	Fe/A/$\overset{*}{C}$
fried, 2 medium tomatoes	140	95	8	4	A/C
Turnips, boiled[Sa], 1 helping	120	17	0	3	Ca/$\overset{*}{C}$

Food, and portion	Wt (g)	En (kcal)	Fat (g)	Fib (g)	Nutrients
Yam, boiled[Sa], 1 helping	130	155	0	5	
Vegetable dishes and products					
Bubble and squeak[Sa], 1 helping	145	185	13	3	C
Cauliflower bhajia[Sa], 1 helping	180	195	16	5	Ca/Fe*/A*/C*
Cauliflower cheese[Sa], 1 helping	165	185	13	2	Pro/Ca*/A/$B_{2,3}$/C
Cauliflower white sauce[Sa], 1 helping	165	90	6	2	Ca/C*
Coleslaw[Sa Su], 1 helping	85	70	5	2	C*
Okra curry[Sa], 1 helping	140	365	35	na	Ca/Fe/A*/$B_{1,3}$/C*
Pakoras[Sa], 1 helping	60	110	5	3	Ca/Fe/A/C
Potato curry[Sa], 1 helping	175	290	16	4	Fe/A/$B_{1,3}$/C
Potato salad[Sa Su], 1 helping	105	140	9	1	C
Ratatouille[Sa], 1 helping	250	190	16	5	Fe/A/$B_{1,3}$/C
Samosa, vegetable[Sa], 2 samosas	110	520	46	3	B_1/C
Sweet and sour red cabbage[Sa Su], 1 helping	105	60	3	3	C
Vegetable curry[Sa], 1 helping	220	400	33	na	Ca/Fe/A*/$B_{1,3}$/C*
Vegetable salad, canned[Sa Su], 1 helping	100	120	8	3	A/C
Yogurt Low-fat varieties					
Natural, 1 small carton	150	80	2	0	Pro/Ca*/B_2
Flavoured[Su], 1 small carton	150	120	1	0	Pro/Ca*/B_2
Fruit[Su], 1 small carton	150	145	2	0	Pro/Ca/B_2
Nut, hazel[Su], 1 small carton	150	160	4	0	Pro/Ca*/$B_{2,3}$

Further Reading

Nutrition and disease

J. W. T. Dickerson and H. A. Lee, *Nutrition in the Clinical Management of Disease*, Edward Arnold, London, 1988

Healthy eating guidelines

DHSS, *Diet and Cardiovascular Disease, Committee on Medical Aspects of Food Policy (COMA)*, Report on Health and Social Subjects, 28, HMSO, London, 1984

W. P. T. James, *A Discussion Paper on Proposals for Nutritional Guidelines for Health Education in Britain*, prepared for the National Advisory Committee on Nutrition Education (NACNE), The Health Education Council, London, 1983

Food poisoning

Good Housekeeping Institute, Fact Sheet, *Food Care at Home*, April 1989 issue

Food additives

M. Hanssen, *E. For Additives*, Thorsons, Wellingborough, 1984

Modified recipes

J. Davies and B. Hammond, *Cooking Explained*, Longman, Harlow, 1988

Food portions

S. Bingham and K. Day, 'Average portion weights of food consumed by a randomly selected British population sample', *Applied Nutrition* 41A, 258–264, 1987

H. Crawley, *Food Portion Sizes*, HMSO, London, 1988

Nutrient content of food

B. Holland, I. D. Unwin and D. H. Buss, *Cereals and Cereal Products*, Third supplement to *McCance and Widdowson, The Composition of Foods* (4th Edition), The Royal Society of Chemistry and the Ministry of Agriculture, Fisheries and Food, London, 1988

A. A. Paul and D. A. T. Southgate, *McCance and Widdowson's The Composition of Foods* (4th Edition), HMSO, London, 1978

S. P. Tan, R. W. Wenlock and R. H. Buss, *Immigrant Foods*, Second supplement to *McCance and Widdowson's The Composition of Foods* (4th Edition), The Royal Society of Chemistry and the Ministry of Agriculture, Fisheries and Food, London, 1985

S. J. Wiles, P. A. Nettleton, A. E. Black and A. A. Paul, 'The nutrient composition of some cooked dishes eaten in Britain: a supplementary food composition table', *Journal of Human Nutrition*, 34, 189–223, 1980

Index